Level D

Mastering Math

Program Consultants

Robert Abbott
Assistant Director of Special Education
Waukegan Community Unit School District No. 60
Waukegan, Illinois

Marie Davis
Principal, McCoy Elementary School
Orange County Public Schools
Orlando, Florida

Monika Spindel
Mathematics Teacher
Austin, Texas

Suzanne H. Stevens
Specialist in Learning Disabilities
Learning Enhancement Consultant
Winston-Salem, North Carolina

STECK-VAUGHN
ELEMENTARY · SECONDARY · ADULT · LIBRARY
A Harcourt Company

www.steck-vaughn.com

Table of Contents

Acknowledgments

Editorial Director
Diane Schnell

Supervising Editor
Donna Rodgers

Assistant Art Director
Cynthia Ellis

Design Manager
Sheryl Cota

Media Researcher
Claudette Landry

Contributing Writers
Brantley Eastman, Diane Crowley, Mary Hill, Louise Marinilli, Harriet Stevens, Susan Murphy, Helen Coleman, Ann McSweeney

Illustration
Holly Cooper: page 30   Jean Helmer: pages 9, 11, 24, 35, 49, 78, 83, 84, 85, 109, 123, 129   Laura Jackson: page 88   Lynn McClain: page 29   Linda Medina: pages 3, 7, 27, 37, 46, 51, 53, 55, 79, 80, 81, 89, 99, 103, 105, 131, clocks

Photography
Cover: (clock, butterfly) ©PhotoDisc; pp. 1, 3, 5, 13, 23, 25, 33 ©PhotoDisc; p. 45 ©Dick Durrance II/The Stock Market; p. 75 ©Tony Freeman/PhotoEdit; pp. 77, 83 ©PhotoDisc; p. 87 CORBIS/Digital Studios; p. 97 ©Jeff Greenberg/PhotoEdit; p. 119 ©PhotoDisc p. 127 Quinn Stewart; Additional photography by: Digital Studios.

Cover Design
Tocquigny Design, Inc.

Place Value Through Ten Thousands

Caleb and his mother hiked near a mountain that is 823 feet tall. Write the height of the mountain in hundreds, tens, and ones.

Solve.

hundreds	tens	ones
104	18	3

▷ Write your own problem. Use a number that has hundreds, tens, and ones.

_____

_____

_____

_____

Hundreds, Tens, and Ones

We write all numbers with these **digits**: 0, 1, 2, 3, 4, 5, 6, 7, 8, and 9.

tens	ones
7	4

7 tens 4 ones

= 74

seventy-four

hundreds	tens	ones
3	4	7

3 hundreds 4 tens 7 ones

= 347

three hundred forty-seven

Guided Practice

▶ Write each missing number.

1. 82 = __8__ tens __2__ ones

2. 35 = _____ tens _____ ones

3. 61 = _____ tens _____ one

4. 14 = _____ ten _____ ones

5. 52 = _____ tens _____ ones

6. 83 = _____ tens _____ ones

7. 187 = _____ hundred _____ tens _____ ones

8. 392 = _____ hundreds _____ tens _____ ones

9. 860 = _____ hundreds _____ tens _____ ones

10. 737 = _____ hundreds _____ tens _____ ones

Practice

▷Write each missing number.

1. 24 = _____ tens _____ ones

2. 44 = _____ tens _____ ones

3. 98 = _____ tens _____ ones

4. 57 = _____ tens _____ ones

5. 17 = _____ ten _____ ones

6. 62 = _____ tens _____ ones

7. 51 = _____ tens _____ one

8. 80 = _____ tens _____ ones

9. 75 = _____ tens _____ ones

10. 39 = _____ tens _____ ones

11. 43 = _____ tens _____ ones

12. 99 = _____ tens _____ ones

13. 117 = _____ hundred _____ ten _____ ones

14. 250 = _____ hundreds _____ tens _____ ones

15. 638 = _____ hundreds _____ tens _____ ones

16. 700 = _____ hundreds _____ tens _____ ones

17. 939 = _____ hundreds _____ tens _____ ones

18. 405 = _____ hundreds _____ tens _____ ones

19. 521 = _____ hundreds _____ tens _____ one

20. 100 = _____ hundred _____ tens _____ones

Using Math

▷The Carvers are buying a new oven. The oven costs $352. Write this price as hundreds, tens, and ones.

_____ hundreds _____ tens _____ ones

Thousands

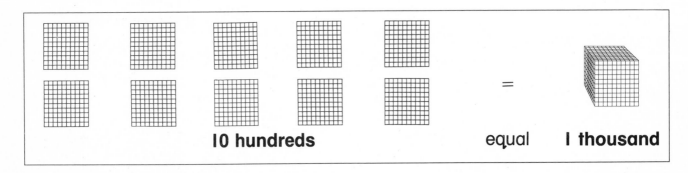

10 hundreds   **equal**   **1 thousand**

thousands	hundreds	tens	ones
2 ,	1	5	8

2 thousands   1 hundred 5 tens 8 ones
two thousand, one hundred fifty-eight

You can write 2 thousands 1 hundred 5 tens 8 ones
   in **expanded form** as ⟶   **2,000 + 100 + 50 + 8**

The **standard form** of 2,000 + 100 + 50 + 8 is ⟶   **2,158**

A **comma** separates the thousands from the hundreds.

Guided Practice

▷ Write each number in standard form.

1. 5,000 + 400 + 60 + 5 = <u>*5,465*</u>   2. 2,000 + 800 + 30 + 9 = _____

3. 3,000 + 600 + 70 + 2 = _____   4. 8,000 + 100 + 20 + 6 = _____

5. 7,000 + 200 + 40 = _____   6. 1,000 + 300 + 80 = _____

7. 6,000 + 900 + 50 = _____   8. 9,000 + 800 + 10 = _____

9. 4,000 + 80 + 2 = _____   10. 5,000 + 40 + 3 = _____

Practice

▷ Write each number in standard form.

1. $4,000 + 600 + 30 + 3 = $ _____   2. $1,000 + 300 + 40 + 8 = $ _____

3. $9,000 + 900 + 20 + 1 = $ _____   4. $600 + 80 + 7 = $ _____

5. $100 + 50 + 9 = $ _____   6. $2,000 + 400 + 8 = $ _____

7. $7,000 + 300 + 20 = $ _____   8. $5,000 + 600 + 10 + 5 = $ _____

9. $2,000 + 500 + 80 + 4 = $ _____   10. $3,000 + 900 + 90 + 9 = $ _____

11. $700 + 20 + 7 = $ _____   12. $8,000 + 600 + 80 + 6 = $ _____

13. $1,000 + 40 + 2 = $ _____   14. $4,000 + 100 + 20 = $ _____

15. $5,000 + 700 + 50 + 3 = $ _____   16. $7,000 + 800 = $ _____

17. $6,000 + 600 + 20 + 2 = $ _____   18. $9,000 + 100 + 40 + 8 = $ _____

19. $8,000 + 900 + 40 = $ _____   20. $3,000 + 50 + 1 = $ _____

Using Math

▷ Karen has saved 1,628 pennies in three years. She wants to put them in jars. A large jar holds 1,000 pennies. A small jar holds 100 pennies.

How many large jars does Karen need for her pennies?

She needs _____ large jar.

How many small jars does Karen need for her pennies?

She needs _____ small jars.

How many pennies will be left?

There will be _____ pennies left.

Ten Thousands

Each digit in a number has a **value.** The value of a digit depends on its **place** in a number.

ten thousands	thousands		hundreds	tens	ones
4	6	,	5	3	8

Look at the place and the value of each underlined digit.

	Digit	Place	Value
<u>4</u> 6, 5 3 8	4	ten thousands	40,000
4 <u>6</u>, 5 3 8	6	thousands	6,000
4 6, <u>5</u> 3 8	5	hundreds	500
4 6, 5 <u>3</u> 8	3	tens	30
4 6, 5 3 <u>8</u>	8	ones	8

$$46{,}538 = 40{,}000 + 6{,}000 + 500 + 30 + 8$$

Guided Practice

▷ Write the value of each underlined digit.

1. 7 <u>5</u>, 8 2 0 *5,000*

2. <u>1</u> 6, 4 3 3 _____

3. <u>3</u>, 2 9 4 _____

4. 8 0, <u>6</u> 9 4 _____

5. 4 7, <u>3</u> 6 0 _____

6. 9, 1 <u>2</u> 5 _____

7. 6 4, 9 2 <u>3</u> _____

8. <u>7</u> 2, 4 0 0 _____

9. <u>8</u>, 7 0 6 _____

10. 5 3, <u>2</u> 8 5 _____

6

Practice

▷ Write the value of each underlined digit.

1. <u>6</u> 2, 8 5 5 _____

2. 7 1, <u>9</u> 4 3 _____

3. 2 <u>5</u>, 7 0 0 _____

4. 8, 6 <u>9</u> 3 _____

5. <u>1</u> 2, 3 3 4 _____

6. 1 0, 4 6 <u>9</u> _____

7. 5, <u>8</u> 9 0 _____

8. 4 <u>4</u>, 3 1 1 _____

9. <u>9</u> 3, 9 0 6 _____

10. 3, <u>6</u> 5 8 _____

11. 2 0, 8 <u>5</u> 1 _____

12. <u>8</u> 0, 9 3 6 _____

13. 6, 7 7 <u>7</u> _____

14. 5 7, <u>5</u> 7 5 _____

15. 7 <u>3</u>, 1 0 0 _____

16. 4, 8 <u>8</u> 9 _____

17. 3 9, <u>6</u> 5 2 _____

18. 1 <u>5</u>, 5 4 0 _____

19. 6 2, 0 0 <u>5</u> _____

20. <u>9</u>, 1 8 3 _____

Using Math

▷ Yesterday, Hamburger King's sign showed it had sold 32,500 hamburgers in one year. Today, 78 hamburgers were sold. Steve is putting the new numbers on the sign. He has five number cards.

| 8 | | 7 | | 2 | | 5 | | 3 |

We have sold ☐ 2 , 5 ☐ 8 Hamburgers!

Steve has put three cards on the sign. Write the missing card numbers in the correct place on the sign.

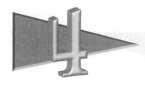

Comparing Numbers

Which number has the greater value: 569 or 573?

When you compare numbers, line up the digits of each number.

Start at the left and compare.

hundreds	tens	ones
5	6	9
5	7	3

●——————→

Step 1 ▶ Compare the hundreds.

5 hundreds are the same as 5 hundreds, so you compare the next digit.

Step 2 ▶ Compare the tens.

7 tens are greater than 6 tens, so **573 is greater than 569.**

> means **is greater than.**
573 > 569   426 > 395

< means **is less than.**
392 < 428   398 < 399

Guided Practice

▶ Ring **greater** or **less**. Then ring > or <.

1. 217 is ⟨greater / **less**⟩ than 271 217 > / ⟨**<**⟩ 271	2. 852 is ⟨greater / less⟩ than 749 852 > / < 749
3. 1,036 is ⟨greater / less⟩ than 1,163 1,036 > / < 1,163	4. 2,168 is ⟨greater / less⟩ than 2,174 2,168 > / < 2,174

Practice

▷Compare. Ring > or <.

1. 944 >/< 494	2. 1,540 >/< 1,539	3. 90,037 >/< 90,377
4. 30,894 >/< 40,894	5. 890 >/< 980	6. 2,165 >/< 1,265
7. 635 >/< 735	8. 4,691 >/< 4,690	9. 89,460 >/< 84,460
10. 268 >/< 258	11. 25,344 >/< 25,434	12. 6,555 >/< 6,565
13. 3,709 >/< 3,708	14. 168 >/< 618	15. 85,183 >/< 58,183
16. 550 >/< 559	17. 7,320 >/< 7,820	18. 399 >/< 400

Using Math

▷In Centerville, there are two schools. South School has 282 students. North School has 289 students. Which school has less students?

_____ has less students.

Rounding to Tens

When you **round** small numbers, you usually go to the nearest ten.

Round 26 to the nearest ten.

Go to 30.

| 20 | 21 | 22 | 23 | 24 | 25 | 26 | 27 | 28 | 29 | 30 |

Round 54 to the nearest ten.

Go back to 50.

| 50 | 51 | 52 | 53 | 54 | 55 | 56 | 57 | 58 | 59 | 60 |

If the ones' digit is **5 or more,** round to the next ten.

Round 35 to the nearest ten.

Go to 40.

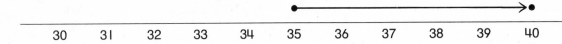

| 30 | 31 | 32 | 33 | 34 | 35 | 36 | 37 | 38 | 39 | 40 |

Guided Practice

▷ Round each number to the nearest ten.

1. 87 _90_

2. 52 ____

3. 22 ____

4. 91 ____

5. 17 ____

6. 63 ____

7. 75 ____

8. 44 ____

9. 36 ____

10. 8 ____

11. 59 ____

12. 72 ____

10

Practice

▷ Round each number to the nearest ten.

1. 14 _____   2. 58 _____   3. 29 _____   4. 75 _____

5. 72 _____   6. 45 _____   7. 93 _____   8. 84 _____

9. 81 _____   10. 66 _____   11. 7 _____   12. 42 _____

13. 25 _____   14. 12 _____   15. 54 _____   16. 88 _____

17. 37 _____   18. 76 _____   19. 19 _____   20. 63 _____

21. 82 _____   22. 65 _____   23. 44 _____   24. 22 _____

25. 91 _____   26. 55 _____   27. 28 _____   28. 67 _____

29. 78 _____   30. 32 _____   31. 64 _____   32. 51 _____

33. 18 _____   34. 48 _____   35. 23 _____   36. 59 _____

37. 34 _____   38. 77 _____   39. 94 _____   40. 35 _____

41. 68 _____   42. 89 _____   43. 46 _____   44. 53 _____

45. 92 _____   46. 33 _____   47. 57 _____   48. 9 _____

Using Math

▷ Pam's father is ordering a cake for her birthday party.
There will be 17 people at the party.
What size cake should Pam's father buy?

He should buy size _____ cake.

Rounding Large Numbers

You learned how to round small numbers. Now you will learn how to round large numbers.

Round 758 to the nearest ten.

| 750 | 751 | 752 | 753 | 754 | 755 | 756 | 757 | 758 | 759 | 760 |

Step 1	Underline the place you are rounding to.	7 5 8
Step 2	Circle the next digit to the right.	7 5 8
Step 3	If the circled digit is **5 or more,** round up to the nearest ten.	7 6 0

Guided Practice

▷Round each number to the nearest ten.

1. 329 _330_

2. 583 _____

3. 2,065 _____

4. 5,879 _____

▷Round each number to the nearest hundred.

5. 863 _900_

6. 5,916 _____

7. 729 _____

8. 10,354 _____

▷Round each number to the nearest thousand.

9. 1,762 _2,000_

10. 24,333 _____

Practice

▷Round each number to the nearest ten.

1. 454 _____

2. 758 _____

3. 2,175 _____

4. 1,975 _____

5. 5,333 _____

6. 114 _____

7. 628 _____

8. 115 _____

9. 3,486 _____

10. 30,562 _____

11. 7,979 _____

12. 848 _____

▷Round each number to the nearest hundred.

13. 460 _____

14. 194 _____

15. 1,542 _____

16. 2,835 _____

17. 3,561 _____

18. 250 _____

19. 752 _____

20. 942 _____

21. 10,164 _____

22. 65,666 _____

23. 8,119 _____

24. 580 _____

▷Round each number to the nearest thousand.

25. 1,232 _____

26. 7,620 _____

27. 32,520 _____

28. 26,589 _____

29. 52,178 _____

30. 4,360 _____

Using Math

▷Ken writes for the school paper. He is writing a story about the Firefighters' Day Fair. There were 2,682 tickets sold for the fair. In his story, Ken rounds the number of tickets sold to the nearest hundred. What number does Ken use in his story?

Ken writes that about _____ tickets were sold.

13

Time to the Minute

There are 12 hours on a clock. Every hour has 60 minutes. Each minute of an hour is shown by a minute mark.

What time is it?

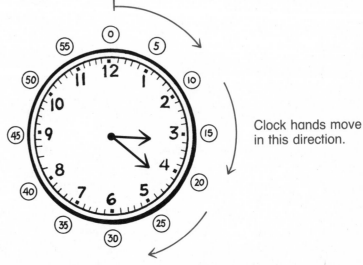

Clock hands move in this direction.

Step 1 Look at the short hand. It is the **hour hand.** It points to 3. The hour is 3.

Step 2 Look at the long hand. It is the **minute hand.** Start at the 12, and count by fives to the number just before the minute hand (5-10-15-20). Then count by ones (20-21-22).

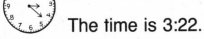

The time is 3:22.

Guided Practice

▷ Write each time.

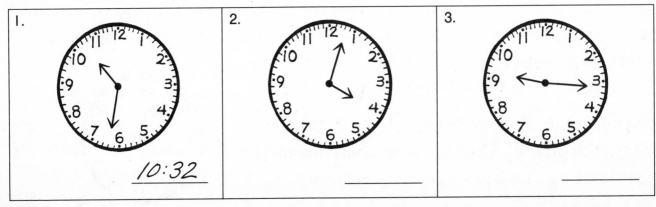

1.	2.	3.
_10:32_	_____	_____

14

Practice

▷ Write each time.

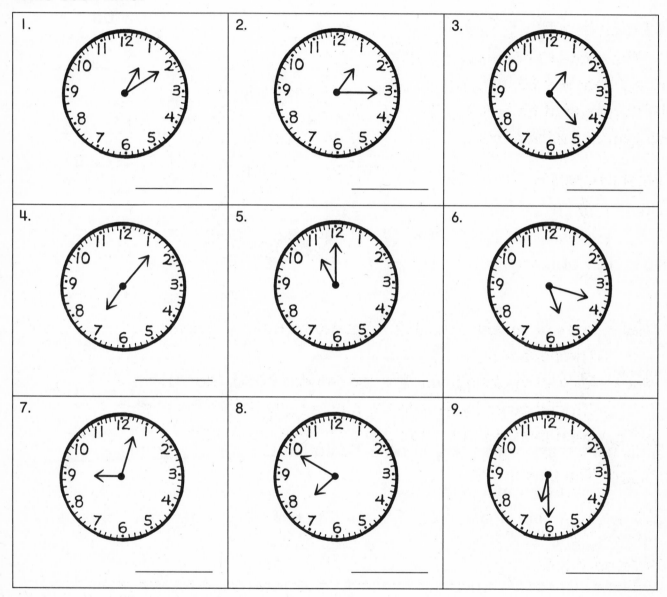

1.	2.	3.
4.	5.	6.
7.	8.	9.

Using Math

▷ The bus stops at Center Street at 11:27. Draw a
minute hand on the clock to show where the minute
hand will be when it is 11:27.

15

Problem Solving

Use a Graph

This *bar graph* shows how much snowfall some cities expect each year.

On this graph, each space shows 10 inches of snow.

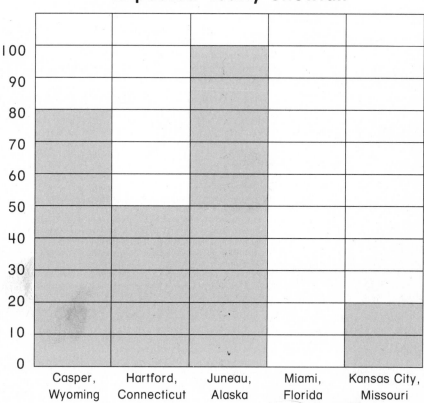

Expected Yearly Snowfall

How many inches of snow can be expected in Casper, Wyoming?

Step 1	Find **Casper** on the graph.
Step 2	With your finger, trace the color bar above Casper to the top.
Step 3	Move your finger left to find the number.

Casper can expect to get ＿＿＿ inches of snowfall.

Guided Practice

▷ Write how many inches of snowfall for each city.

1. ＿＿＿ Hartford, Connecticut   2. ＿＿＿ Juneau, Alaska

3. ＿＿＿ Miami, Florida   4. ＿＿＿ Kansas City, Missouri

16

Practice

Mrs. Bruce made this graph to show how many books were ordered through the student book club.

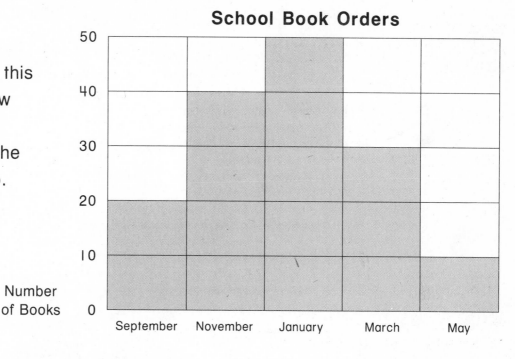

School Book Orders

Number of Books

▶Use the graph to answer the questions.

1. In which month were the most books ordered?

_____

2. In which month were the fewest books ordered?

_____

3. In which month were 40 books ordered?

_____

4. In which month were 30 books ordered?

_____

▶Use the graph to solve.

5. How many more books were ordered in January than in March?

6. How many more books were ordered in March than in September?

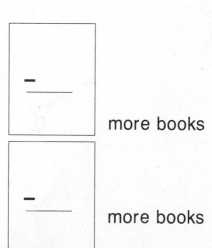

_____ − _____ more books

_____ − _____ more books

17

▷ Write each missing number.   pages 2–3

1. 86 = _____ tens _____ ones

2. 42 = _____ tens _____ ones

3. 15 = _____ ten _____ ones

4. 79 = _____ tens _____ ones

5. 231 = _____ hundreds _____ tens _____ one

6. 450 = _____ hundreds _____ tens _____ ones

▷ Write each number in standard form.   pages 4–5

7. 600 + 80 + 3 = _____

8. 100 + 70 + 1 = _____

9. 2,000 + 900 + 40 + 4 = _____

10. 5,000 + 20 + 8 = _____

▷ Write the value of each underlined digit.   pages 6–7

11. <u>6</u>, 8 4 0 _____

12. 9, <u>1</u> 5 3 _____

13. <u>5</u> 2, 7 1 4 _____

14. 3 <u>3</u>, 9 4 5 _____

15. 7 0, 9 <u>5</u> 0 _____

16. 1 8, 2 2 <u>6</u> _____

▷ Compare. Ring > or <.   pages 8–9

17. 121 $\frac{>}{<}$ 112	18. 569 $\frac{>}{<}$ 659	19. 83,122 $\frac{>}{<}$ 84,220
20. 3,450 $\frac{>}{<}$ 3,452	21. 45,710 $\frac{>}{<}$ 45,709	22. 635 $\frac{>}{<}$ 536

 **CHAPTER** **1** **Review**

▷ Round each number to the nearest ten. pages 10–11

23. 32 _____   24. 78 _____   25. 41 _____

26. 53 _____   27. 65 _____   28. 86 _____

▷ Round each number to the nearest ten. pages 12–13

29. 356 _____   30. 642 _____   31. 3,571 _____

32. 1,081 _____   33. 7,455 _____   34. 162 _____

▷ Round each number to the nearest hundred. pages 12–13

35. 581 _____   36. 242 _____   37. 44,172 _____

38. 3,803 _____   39. 9,696 _____   40. 768 _____

▷ Round each number to the nearest thousand. pages 12–13

41. 5,981 _____   42. 7,542 _____   43. 35,166 _____

44. 17,400 _____   45. 82,613 _____   46. 2,257 _____

▷ Write each time. pages 14–15

47.	48.	49.
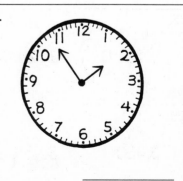		

_____   _____   _____

Ms. Dale buys items for the library.

She makes this graph to show what she has bought.

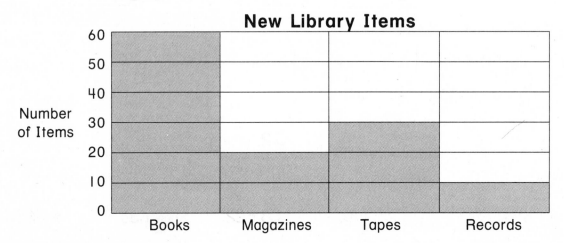

▷ Look at the graph.

Write how many items.

pages 16–17

50. _____ Books	51. _____ Tapes

▷ Use the graph to answer.

52. What item did Ms. Dale buy most? _____	53. What item did Ms. Dale buy least? _____
54. How many more books did Ms. Dale buy than magazines? _____ more books	55. How many more tapes did Ms. Dale buy than records? _____ more tapes

▷Write each missing number.

1. 27 = _____ tens _____ ones   2. 53 = _____ tens _____ ones

▷Write each number in standard form.

3. 800 + 30 + 6 = _____   4. 4,000 + 500 + 30 = _____

▷Write the value of each underlined digit.

5. <u>9</u>, 8 6 3 _____   6. <u>5</u> 2, 0 3 1 _____

▷Compare. Ring > or <.

7. 9,653 $\genfrac{}{}{0pt}{}{>}{<}$ 9,643   8. 38,622 $\genfrac{}{}{0pt}{}{>}{<}$ 38,822   9. 8,633 $\genfrac{}{}{0pt}{}{>}{<}$ 9,833

▷Round each number to the nearest ten.

10. 72 _____   11. 455 _____   12. 157 _____

▷Round each number to the nearest hundred.

13. 780 _____   14. 3,829 _____   15. 564 _____

▷Round each number to the nearest thousand.

16. 4,582 _____   17. 73,391 _____   18. 6,633 _____

▷Write each time.

19.	20.	21.
	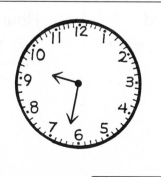	
_____	_____	_____

21

Sarah saves coins in a jar. She made this graph after she counted them. It shows how many coins she has.

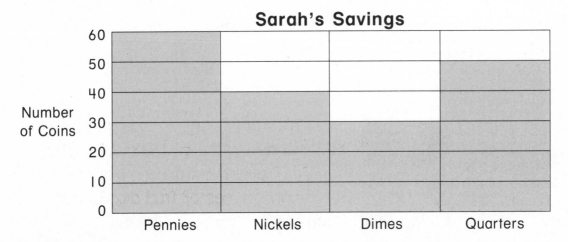

Sarah's Savings

▷ Look at the graph.
Write how many items.

22. _____ Pennies	23. _____ Quarters

▷ Use the graph to answer.

24. What coin has Sarah saved the most? _____	25. What coin has Sarah saved the least? _____
26. How many more pennies than nickels did Sarah save? _____ more pennies	27. How many more quarters than dimes did Sarah save? _____ more quarters

2 Addition and Subtraction

▽ ▽ ▽ ▽ ▽ ▽ ▽

Sondra's mom bought some grapefruit and oranges at the grocery store. She bought 12 grapefruit and 12 oranges. How many pieces of fruit did Sondra's mom buy?

Solve.

▷ Write a problem about buying something you like at the grocery store.

_____

_____

_____

_____

Adding to 18

You add to find out how many there are in all.

How many helmets are there in all?

Add: 6 helmets + 5 helmets = 11 helmets in all.

Write: 6 + 5 = 11   or $\begin{array}{r} 6 \\ +5 \\ \hline 11 \end{array}$

The numbers you add are called **addends.** 6 and 5 are addends.

The answer is called the **sum.** 11 is the sum.

Guided Practice

▷ Add.

1. $\begin{array}{r} 2 \\ +5 \\ \hline 7 \end{array}$	2. $\begin{array}{r} 7 \\ +2 \\ \hline \end{array}$	3. $\begin{array}{r} 6 \\ +6 \\ \hline \end{array}$	4. $\begin{array}{r} 3 \\ +8 \\ \hline \end{array}$
5. 3 + 0 =	6. 5 + 8 =	7. 9 + 9 =	8. 2 + 4 =

Practice

▷ Add.

1. $\begin{array}{r} 3 \\ + 6 \\ \hline \end{array}$	2. $\begin{array}{r} 4 \\ + 4 \\ \hline \end{array}$	3. $\begin{array}{r} 7 \\ + 3 \\ \hline \end{array}$	4. $\begin{array}{r} 4 \\ + 8 \\ \hline \end{array}$
5. $\begin{array}{r} 5 \\ + 6 \\ \hline \end{array}$	6. $\begin{array}{r} 6 \\ + 9 \\ \hline \end{array}$	7. $\begin{array}{r} 8 \\ + 7 \\ \hline \end{array}$	8. $\begin{array}{r} 5 \\ + 8 \\ \hline \end{array}$
9. $\begin{array}{r} 7 \\ + 6 \\ \hline \end{array}$	10. $\begin{array}{r} 8 \\ + 8 \\ \hline \end{array}$	11. $\begin{array}{r} 9 \\ + 7 \\ \hline \end{array}$	12. $\begin{array}{r} 6 \\ + 5 \\ \hline \end{array}$
13. $4 + 5 =$	14. $5 + 5 =$	15. $7 + 7 =$	16. $5 + 7 =$

Using Math

▷ A bike shop has 7 ten-speed bikes and 6 dirt bikes. How many bikes are there in all?

There are _____ bikes in all.

Work here.

Adding 2-Digit Numbers

Step 1 Add the ones.

Step 2 Add the tens.

tens	ones
4	6
+ 1	2
5	8

Sometimes you need to **regroup** to add.

Step 1 Add the ones.

7 ones + 5 ones = 12 ones

Regroup 12 ones as 1 ten 2 ones.

Write 2 in the ones' place.

Write 1 in the tens' column.

tens	ones
1	
4	7
+ 2	5
7	2

Step 2 Add the tens.

Guided Practice

▷ Add.

1.	2.	3.	4.	5.
1 27 + 46 73	13 + 24	15 + 25	39 + 30	46 + 38

Practice

▷ Add.

1. $\begin{array}{r} 13 \\ +28 \\ \hline \end{array}$	2. $\begin{array}{r} 15 \\ +78 \\ \hline \end{array}$	3. $\begin{array}{r} 26 \\ +24 \\ \hline \end{array}$	4. $\begin{array}{r} 34 \\ +46 \\ \hline \end{array}$	5. $\begin{array}{r} 16 \\ +36 \\ \hline \end{array}$
6. $\begin{array}{r} 22 \\ +17 \\ \hline \end{array}$	7. $\begin{array}{r} 53 \\ +19 \\ \hline \end{array}$	8. $\begin{array}{r} 29 \\ +31 \\ \hline \end{array}$	9. $\begin{array}{r} 29 \\ +12 \\ \hline \end{array}$	10. $\begin{array}{r} 33 \\ +58 \\ \hline \end{array}$
11. $\begin{array}{r} 17 \\ +42 \\ \hline \end{array}$	12. $\begin{array}{r} 25 \\ +67 \\ \hline \end{array}$	13. $\begin{array}{r} 26 \\ +41 \\ \hline \end{array}$	14. $\begin{array}{r} 13 \\ +27 \\ \hline \end{array}$	15. $\begin{array}{r} 21 \\ +49 \\ \hline \end{array}$

Using Math

▷ Maria took her brother to the toy store. She bought him a balloon for 35¢ and a sticker for 15¢. How much did Maria spend?

Maria spent _____ ¢.

Work here.

27

Adding 3- and 4-Digit Numbers

Sometimes when you add large numbers, you regroup more than one time.

| Step 1 | Add the ones. Regroup 12 ones as 1 ten 2 ones. |

hundreds	tens	ones
1	1	
6	8	9
+ 2	7	3
9	6	2

| Step 2 | Add the tens. Regroup 16 tens as 1 hundred 6 tens. |

| Step 3 | Add the hundreds. |

Guided Practice

▷ Add.

1.　　1 1 　　131 　+289 　420	2.　　467 　+133	3.　　328 　+492
5.　　464 　+235	6.　　1,251 　+ 670	7.　　7,096 　+ 1,930

4.
4.　　3,612 　+ 556
8.　　758 　+764

28

Practice

Add.

1. $\begin{array}{r} 129 \\ +\ 663 \\ \hline \end{array}$	2. $\begin{array}{r} 429 \\ +\ 169 \\ \hline \end{array}$	3. $\begin{array}{r} 338 \\ +\ 525 \\ \hline \end{array}$	4. $\begin{array}{r} 817 \\ +\ 156 \\ \hline \end{array}$	5. $\begin{array}{r} 4,175 \\ +\ \ \ 912 \\ \hline \end{array}$
6. $\begin{array}{r} 129 \\ +\ 344 \\ \hline \end{array}$	7. $\begin{array}{r} 176 \\ +\ 619 \\ \hline \end{array}$	8. $\begin{array}{r} 693 \\ +\ 258 \\ \hline \end{array}$	9. $\begin{array}{r} 126 \\ +\ 639 \\ \hline \end{array}$	10. $\begin{array}{r} 5,856 \\ +\ 1,541 \\ \hline \end{array}$
11. $\begin{array}{r} 268 \\ +\ 231 \\ \hline \end{array}$	12. $\begin{array}{r} 375 \\ +\ 550 \\ \hline \end{array}$	13. $\begin{array}{r} 1,345 \\ +\ 2,175 \\ \hline \end{array}$	14. $\begin{array}{r} 536 \\ +\ 161 \\ \hline \end{array}$	15. $\begin{array}{r} 759 \\ +\ 122 \\ \hline \end{array}$

Using Math

The rodeo was in town for two days. The first day, 367 people came to see the show. The second day, 385 people were there. How many people saw the rodeo?

_____ people saw the rodeo.

Work here.

Subtraction Facts Through 18

You subtract to find out how many are left.

How many hawks are left?

Subtract: 5 hawks − 3 hawks = 2 hawks.

Write: 5 − 3 = 2   or
$$\begin{array}{r} 5 \\ -\ 3 \\ \hline 2 \end{array}$$

The answer to a subtraction problem is called the **difference**.

2 is the difference.

Guided Practice

▷ Subtract.

1. $\begin{array}{r} 7 \\ -\ 4 \\ \hline 3 \end{array}$	2. $\begin{array}{r} 9 \\ -\ 6 \\ \hline \end{array}$	3. $\begin{array}{r} 8 \\ -\ 3 \\ \hline \end{array}$	4. $\begin{array}{r} 10 \\ -\ 5 \\ \hline \end{array}$
5. 11 − 5 =	6. 18 − 9 =	7. 12 − 6 =	8. 13 − 8 =

Practice

▷Subtract.

1. $\begin{array}{r} 15 \\ -\ 9 \\ \hline \end{array}$	2. $\begin{array}{r} 9 \\ -\ 0 \\ \hline \end{array}$	3. $\begin{array}{r} 11 \\ -\ 5 \\ \hline \end{array}$	4. $\begin{array}{r} 10 \\ -\ 2 \\ \hline \end{array}$	5. $\begin{array}{r} 14 \\ -\ 9 \\ \hline \end{array}$
6. $\begin{array}{r} 9 \\ -\ 5 \\ \hline \end{array}$	7. $\begin{array}{r} 12 \\ -\ 7 \\ \hline \end{array}$	8. $\begin{array}{r} 15 \\ -\ 8 \\ \hline \end{array}$	9. $\begin{array}{r} 11 \\ -\ 9 \\ \hline \end{array}$	10. $\begin{array}{r} 16 \\ -\ 8 \\ \hline \end{array}$
11. $\begin{array}{r} 13 \\ -\ 7 \\ \hline \end{array}$	12. $\begin{array}{r} 8 \\ -\ 3 \\ \hline \end{array}$	13. $\begin{array}{r} 7 \\ -\ 4 \\ \hline \end{array}$	14. $\begin{array}{r} 14 \\ -\ 5 \\ \hline \end{array}$	15. $\begin{array}{r} 17 \\ -\ 9 \\ \hline \end{array}$

16. $18 - 9 =$	17. $16 - 9 =$	18. $17 - 8 =$	19. $12 - 4 =$

Problem Solving

▷Who sold the most tickets?

_____ sold the most tickets.

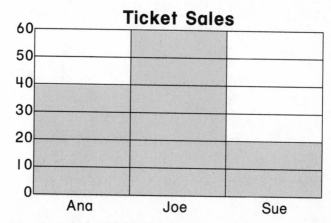

Ticket Sales

Number of Tickets

Ana   Joe   Sue

31

Subtracting 2-Digit Numbers

| Step 1 | Subtract the ones. |

| Step 2 | Subtract the tens. |

	tens	ones
	4	5
−	1	3
	3	2

Sometimes you need to **regroup** when you subtract.

| Step 1 | Can you subtract the ones? No. Regroup 4 tens 2 ones as 3 tens 12 ones. Now subtract the ones. |

	tens	ones
	$\overset{3}{\cancel{4}}$	$\overset{12}{\cancel{2}}$
−	1	5
	2	7

| Step 2 | Subtract the tens. |

Guided Practice

▷ Subtract.

1.	2.	3.	4.	5.
$\overset{5\ 10}{\cancel{6}\cancel{0}}$ − 32 = 28	44 − 26	46 − 26	37 − 18	24 − 18

32

Practice

Subtract.

1. $\begin{array}{r}15\\-13\\\hline\end{array}$	2. $\begin{array}{r}55\\-22\\\hline\end{array}$	3. $\begin{array}{r}60\\-32\\\hline\end{array}$	4. $\begin{array}{r}44\\-26\\\hline\end{array}$	5. $\begin{array}{r}97\\-38\\\hline\end{array}$
6. $\begin{array}{r}90\\-73\\\hline\end{array}$	7. $\begin{array}{r}84\\-76\\\hline\end{array}$	8. $\begin{array}{r}24\\-18\\\hline\end{array}$	9. $\begin{array}{r}52\\-24\\\hline\end{array}$	10. $\begin{array}{r}47\\-16\\\hline\end{array}$
11. $\begin{array}{r}21\\-14\\\hline\end{array}$	12. $\begin{array}{r}79\\-58\\\hline\end{array}$	13. $\begin{array}{r}57\\-49\\\hline\end{array}$	14. $\begin{array}{r}28\\-19\\\hline\end{array}$	15. $\begin{array}{r}55\\-28\\\hline\end{array}$

Using Math

Mr. Wilson had 54 cows in the pasture by the barn. He moved 28 of the cows to another pasture. How many cows were left in the pasture by the barn?

There were _____ cows left.

Work here.

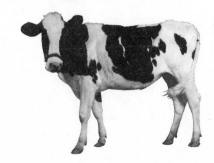

Subtracting 3- and 4-Digit Numbers

Sometimes when you subtract large numbers, you regroup more
than one time.

Step 1 Can you subtract the ones? No.
Regroup 4 tens 2 ones as
3 tens 12 ones.
Now subtract the ones.

Step 2 Can you subtract the tens? No.
Regroup 5 hundreds 3 tens as
4 hundreds 13 tens.
Now subtract the tens.

Step 3 Subtract the hundreds.

hundreds	tens	ones
4	13 $\cancel{3}$	12
$\cancel{5}$	$\cancel{4}$	$\cancel{2}$
$-$ 1	6	8
3	7	4

Guided Practice

▷ Subtract.

1. $\begin{array}{r} \overset{11}{4}\,\overset{}{\cancel{5}}\,\overset{13}{\cancel{3}} \\ 5\,2\,3 \\ -\ 3\,6\,4 \\ \hline 1\,5\,9 \end{array}$	2. $\begin{array}{r} 346 \\ -\ 178 \\ \hline \end{array}$	3. $\begin{array}{r} 4{,}349 \\ -\ 1{,}678 \\ \hline \end{array}$	4. $\begin{array}{r} 864 \\ -\ 478 \\ \hline \end{array}$
5. $\begin{array}{r} 958 \\ -\ 646 \\ \hline \end{array}$	6. $\begin{array}{r} 1{,}564 \\ -\ 782 \\ \hline \end{array}$	7. $\begin{array}{r} 807 \\ -\ 756 \\ \hline \end{array}$	8. $\begin{array}{r} 687 \\ -\ 296 \\ \hline \end{array}$

Practice

▷Subtract.

1. 640 − 126	2. 502 − 192	3. 319 − 121	4. 930 − 369	5. 1,782 − 891
6. 790 − 328	7. 350 − 174	8. 596 − 285	9. 852 − 485	10. 2,154 − 1,972
11. 351 − 181	12. 457 − 128	13. 324 − 175	14. 344 − 285	15. 8,238 − 2,573

Using Math

▷Grover School had Cookout Day. The parents helped cook the food. They cooked 235 hot dogs. In one hour, 196 hot dogs were eaten. How many hot dogs were left?

There were _____ hot dogs left.

Work here.

Time After the Hour

When the minute hand points to the 12, it is the hour. As the minute hand moves around the clock, each minute mark is **after the hour.**

What time is it?

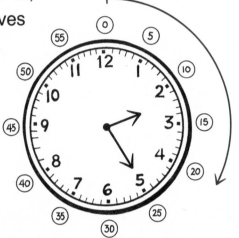

after the hour

Step 1 Look at the hour hand. It is between 2 and 3. The smaller number is the hour. The hour is 2.

Step 2 Look at the minute hand. Count by fives to the minute hand. It is 25 minutes **after the hour.**

The time is 2:25.
You can also say 25 minutes after 2.

Guided Practice

▷Write each time two ways.

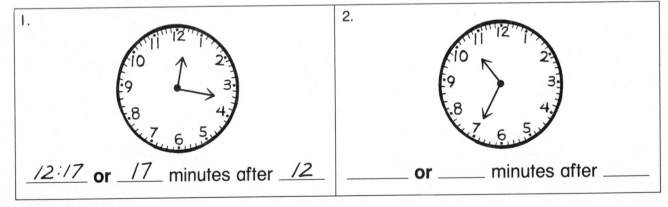

1.	2.
_12:17_ **or** _17_ minutes after _12_	_____ **or** _____ minutes after _____

36

Practice

▷ Write each time two ways.

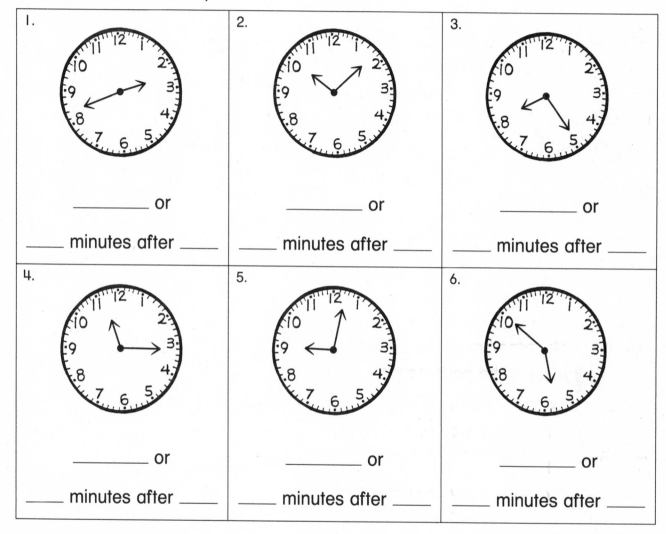

1.

_____ or

_____ minutes after _____

2.

_____ or

_____ minutes after _____

3.

_____ or

_____ minutes after _____

4.

_____ or

_____ minutes after _____

5.

_____ or

_____ minutes after _____

6.

_____ or

_____ minutes after _____

Using Math

▷ The softball game begins at 20 minutes after 4. Rick arrived at the game at 4:25. Was Rick early or late for the game?

Ring your answer.   early   late

 **Problem Solving**

Make a Bar Graph

Akimi Music Store made this table.
It shows how many instruments
are rented each year.

You can use facts from this table
to make a bar graph.

Instruments Rented		
Flutes		20
Clarinets		40
Trumpets		30
Saxophones		10
Trombones		10

Step 1 Find the number of flutes in the table.

<u>20</u> Flutes

Step 2 Find **Flutes** on the graph below.

Step 3 Color the spaces above **Flutes** in the graph
up to the line marked 20.

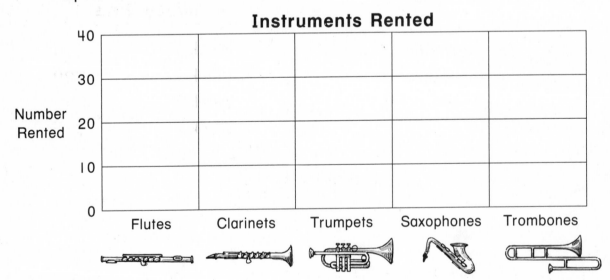

Guided Practice

▷Use the table at the top of this page.
Color the graph to show how many of each instrument.

Practice

▷ Use each table to make a graph.

Favorite Campgrounds	
Pine Lake	2
Blue Mountain	6
Sand Beach	4
Beech Pond	8

1. The scout leaders asked the scouts to choose their favorite campground. This table shows their answers.

Favorite Campgrounds

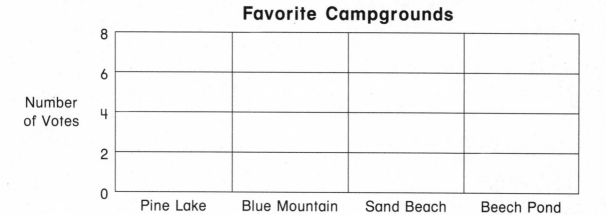

Money Saved	
Week 1	$10
Week 2	$20
Week 3	$40
Week 4	$30

2. The scout troop raised money for the camping trip. This table shows how much money the troop made each week.

Money Saved

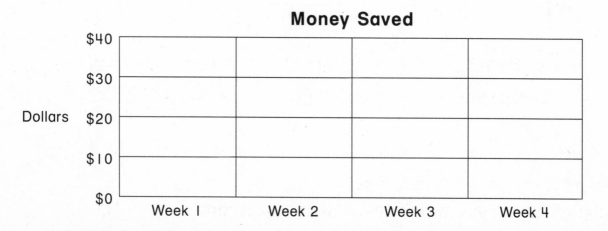

▷Add.

pages 24–25			
1. $\quad$ 9 $+\ 4$	2. $\quad$ 8 $+\ 6$	3. $\quad$ 7 $+\ 9$	4. $\quad$ 5 $+\ 7$
pages 26–27			
5. $\quad$ 36 $+\ 24$	6. $\quad$ 24 $+\ 12$	7. $\quad$ 69 $+\ 27$	8. $\quad$ 46 $+\ 27$
9. $\quad$ 53 $+\ 29$	10. $\quad$ 76 $+\ 14$	11. $\quad$ 13 $+\ 48$	12. $\quad$ 28 $+\ 16$
pages 28–29			
13. $\quad$ 683 $+\ 298$	14. $\quad$ 549 $+\ 151$	15. $\quad$ 868 $+\ 456$	16. $\quad$ 1,963 $+\ 3,741$
17. $\quad$ 6,187 $+\quad 840$	18. $\quad$ 419 $+\ 383$	19. $\quad$ 4,753 $+\quad 465$	20. $\quad$ 246 $+\ 399$

▷Subtract.

pages 30–31			
21. $\quad$ 12 $-\ 4$	22. $\quad$ 16 $-\ 7$	23. $\quad$ 11 $-\ 5$	24. $\quad$ 17 $-\ 9$

**Review**

▷ Subtract.

pages 32–33

25. $\begin{array}{r} 82 \\ -\ 60 \\ \hline \end{array}$	26. $\begin{array}{r} 67 \\ -\ 24 \\ \hline \end{array}$	27. $\begin{array}{r} 53 \\ -\ 37 \\ \hline \end{array}$	28. $\begin{array}{r} 42 \\ -\ 17 \\ \hline \end{array}$
29. $\begin{array}{r} 83 \\ -\ 46 \\ \hline \end{array}$	30. $\begin{array}{r} 71 \\ -\ 23 \\ \hline \end{array}$	31. $\begin{array}{r} 64 \\ -\ 25 \\ \hline \end{array}$	32. $\begin{array}{r} 35 \\ -\ 17 \\ \hline \end{array}$

pages 34–35

33. $\begin{array}{r} 450 \\ -\ 174 \\ \hline \end{array}$	34. $\begin{array}{r} 642 \\ -\ 386 \\ \hline \end{array}$	35. $\begin{array}{r} 1,673 \\ -\ \ \ 891 \\ \hline \end{array}$	36. $\begin{array}{r} 5,226 \\ -\ 1,862 \\ \hline \end{array}$
37. $\begin{array}{r} 5,258 \\ -\ 1,687 \\ \hline \end{array}$	38. $\begin{array}{r} 652 \\ -\ 293 \\ \hline \end{array}$	39. $\begin{array}{r} 2,452 \\ -\ \ \ 672 \\ \hline \end{array}$	40. $\begin{array}{r} 944 \\ -\ 275 \\ \hline \end{array}$

▷ Write each time two ways.   pages 36–37

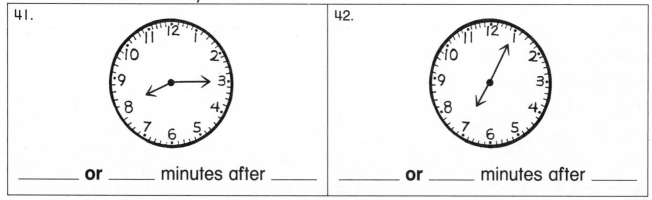

41. _____ **or** _____ minutes after _____

42. _____ **or** _____ minutes after _____

▷Use each table to make a graph.
pages 38–39

43. Students in Science Class A
planted trees in their town.
The table shows how many trees
they planted on each street.

Trees Planted by Class A	
Park Street	8
Main Street	6
High Street	2
Oak Street	4

Trees Planted

44. This table shows the
number of trees
planted by each class.

Trees Planted by Each Class	
Class A	20 trees
Class B	30 trees
Class C	10 trees
Class D	40 trees

Trees Planted by Each Class

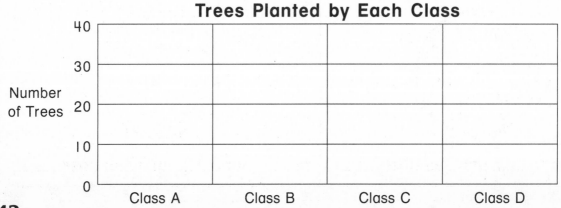

▷Add.

1. 8 + 8	2. 9 + 6	3. 62 + 23	4. 35 + 48
5. 57 + 37	6. 496 + 326	7. 351 + 589	8. 3,692 + 2,842

▷Subtract.

9. 14 − 7	10. 18 − 9	11. 58 − 14	12. 95 − 67
13. 72 − 53	14. 343 − 196	15. 925 − 878	16. 1,519 − 691

▷Write each time two ways.

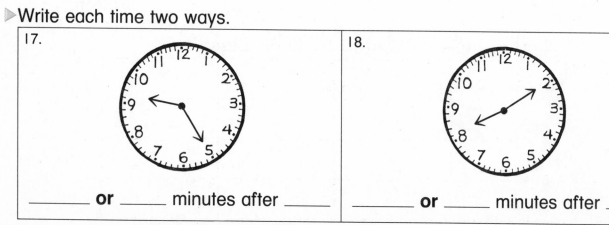

17.	18.
_____ **or** _____ minutes after _____	_____ **or** _____ minutes after _____

▷Use each table to make a graph.

19. The table shows the number of new students in each grade at Smithville School this month.

New Students	
Grade 3	4
Grade 4	6
Grade 5	8
Grade 6	2

New Students

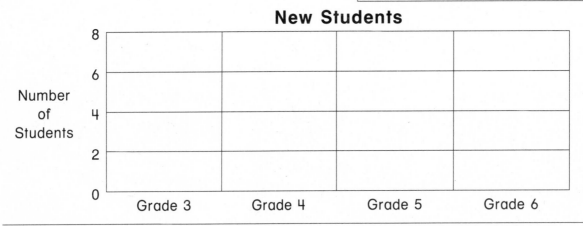

20. The table shows the number of new houses built each month in Smithville.

New Houses	
January	10
April	40
July	30
October	20

New Houses

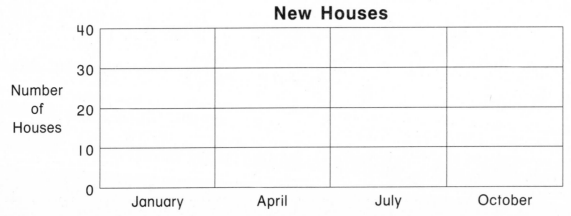

3 Multiplication Facts Through 9

▼ ▼ ▼ ▼ ▼ ▼ ▼

Kamal saw 7 hot air balloons that were taking off for a race. There were 2 people in each balloon basket. How many people in all were in the hot air balloon baskets?

Solve.

Write a problem about a different kind of race.

Multiplying by 0, 1, and 2

You can add to find how many in all. When the groups are equal,
you can also **multiply** to find how many in all.

 $1 + 1 = 2$

$$\begin{array}{r} 2 \\ \times\ 1 \\ \hline 2 \end{array}$$

$1 \times 2 = 2$

 $1 + 1 + 1 = 3$

$$\begin{array}{r} 3 \\ \times\ 1 \\ \hline 3 \end{array}$$

$1 \times 3 = 3$

1 × any number = that number

$0 + 0 = 0$

$$\begin{array}{r} 2 \\ \times\ 0 \\ \hline 0 \end{array}$$

$0 \times 2 = 0$

$0 + 0 + 0 = 0$

$$\begin{array}{r} 3 \\ \times\ 0 \\ \hline 0 \end{array}$$

$0 \times 3 = 0$

0 × any number = 0

$3 + 3 = 6$

$$\begin{array}{r} 3 \\ \times\ 2 \\ \hline 6 \end{array}$$

$2 \times 3 = 6$

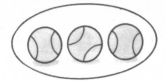
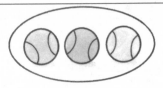

Guided Practice

▷ Multiply.

1. $$\begin{array}{r} 6 \\ \times\ 1 \\ \hline 6 \end{array}$$ 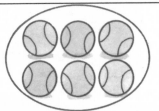	**2.** $$\begin{array}{r} 4 \\ \times\ 2 \\ \hline \end{array}$$ 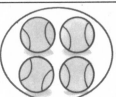
3. $1 \times 5 =$	**4.** $2 \times 2 =$ **5.** $0 \times 5 =$

Practice

▷ Multiply.

1. $\begin{array}{r} 8 \\ \times\,0 \\ \hline \end{array}$	2. $\begin{array}{r} 9 \\ \times\,1 \\ \hline \end{array}$	3. $\begin{array}{r} 7 \\ \times\,0 \\ \hline \end{array}$	4. $\begin{array}{r} 6 \\ \times\,2 \\ \hline \end{array}$	5. $\begin{array}{r} 9 \\ \times\,0 \\ \hline \end{array}$
6. $\begin{array}{r} 1 \\ \times\,1 \\ \hline \end{array}$	7. $\begin{array}{r} 2 \\ \times\,0 \\ \hline \end{array}$	8. $\begin{array}{r} 3 \\ \times\,2 \\ \hline \end{array}$	9. $\begin{array}{r} 9 \\ \times\,2 \\ \hline \end{array}$	10. $\begin{array}{r} 8 \\ \times\,1 \\ \hline \end{array}$
11. $\begin{array}{r} 6 \\ \times\,0 \\ \hline \end{array}$	12. $\begin{array}{r} 8 \\ \times\,2 \\ \hline \end{array}$	13. $\begin{array}{r} 7 \\ \times\,1 \\ \hline \end{array}$	14. $\begin{array}{r} 5 \\ \times\,2 \\ \hline \end{array}$	15. $\begin{array}{r} 1 \\ \times\,2 \\ \hline \end{array}$

16. $2 \times 1 =$	17. $0 \times 6 =$	18. $1 \times 3 =$	19. $2 \times 7 =$

Using Math

▷ There are 2 tennis courts in the park. 4 players are on each court. How many players are there in all?

There are _____ players in all.

Work here.

47

Multiplying by 3 and 4

Add to find the number of dots. Then multiply.

Add. 2 + 2 + 2 = 6

Multiply. $\underset{\text{factors}}{3 \times 2} = \underset{\text{product}}{6}$ or $\begin{array}{r} 2 \\ \times 3 \\ \hline 6 \end{array}$

Add. 2 + 2 + 2 + 2 = 8

Multiply. $4 \times 2 = 8$ or $\begin{array}{r} 2 \\ \times 4 \\ \hline 8 \end{array}$

The numbers we multiply are called **factors.** 4 and 2 are factors.

The answer is called the **product.** 8 is the product.

Guided Practice

▷Multiply.

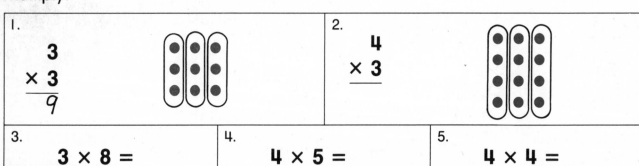

1. $\begin{array}{r} 3 \\ \times 3 \\ \hline 9 \end{array}$	2. $\begin{array}{r} 4 \\ \times 3 \\ \hline \end{array}$
3. $3 \times 8 =$	4. $4 \times 5 =$	5. $4 \times 4 =$

Practice

▷ Multiply.

1. $\begin{array}{r} 6 \\ \times\ 3 \\ \hline \end{array}$	2. $\begin{array}{r} 5 \\ \times\ 3 \\ \hline \end{array}$	3. $\begin{array}{r} 9 \\ \times\ 4 \\ \hline \end{array}$	4. $\begin{array}{r} 8 \\ \times\ 4 \\ \hline \end{array}$	5. $\begin{array}{r} 6 \\ \times\ 4 \\ \hline \end{array}$
6. $\begin{array}{r} 1 \\ \times\ 4 \\ \hline \end{array}$	7. $\begin{array}{r} 0 \\ \times\ 3 \\ \hline \end{array}$	8. $\begin{array}{r} 3 \\ \times\ 4 \\ \hline \end{array}$	9. $\begin{array}{r} 7 \\ \times\ 4 \\ \hline \end{array}$	10. $\begin{array}{r} 9 \\ \times\ 3 \\ \hline \end{array}$
11. $\begin{array}{r} 7 \\ \times\ 3 \\ \hline \end{array}$	12. $\begin{array}{r} 2 \\ \times\ 4 \\ \hline \end{array}$	13. $\begin{array}{r} 8 \\ \times\ 3 \\ \hline \end{array}$	14. $\begin{array}{r} 2 \\ \times\ 3 \\ \hline \end{array}$	15. $\begin{array}{r} 0 \\ \times\ 4 \\ \hline \end{array}$

16. $4 \times 9 =$	17. $3 \times 9 =$	18. $4 \times 0 =$	19. $3 \times 1 =$

Problem Solving

▷ This table shows the favorite hobbies of sixty students.
Use the table to make the graph.

Favorite Hobbies

Favorite Hobbies	
Models	20
Computers	30
Drawing	10

Number of Students

	Models	Computers	Drawing
30			
20			
10			
0			

49

Multiplying by 5 and 6

You can memorize the multiplication facts for 5 and 6 by studying the **multiplication tables.**

Multiplying by 5

×	0	1	2	3	4	5	6	7	8	9
5	0	5	10	15	20	25	30	35	40	45

$5 \times 6 = 30$

$$\begin{array}{r} 6 \\ \times 5 \\ \hline 30 \end{array}$$

Multiplying by 6

×	0	1	2	3	4	5	6	7	8	9
6	0	6	12	18	24	30	36	42	48	54

$6 \times 5 = 30$

$$\begin{array}{r} 5 \\ \times 6 \\ \hline 30 \end{array}$$

> The order of the factors does not change the product.
> $5 \times 6 = 30$ and $6 \times 5 = 30$

Guided Practice

▶ Multiply.

1. $\begin{array}{r} 2 \\ \times 5 \\ \hline 10 \end{array}$	2. $\begin{array}{r} 3 \\ \times 6 \\ \hline \end{array}$	3. $\begin{array}{r} 7 \\ \times 5 \\ \hline \end{array}$	4. $\begin{array}{r} 9 \\ \times 6 \\ \hline \end{array}$
5. $5 \times 3 =$	6. $6 \times 2 =$	7. $6 \times 8 =$	8. $5 \times 6 =$

50

Practice

▷ Multiply.

1. $\begin{array}{r} 4 \\ \times\,5 \\ \hline \end{array}$	2. $\begin{array}{r} 6 \\ \times\,6 \\ \hline \end{array}$	3. $\begin{array}{r} 0 \\ \times\,6 \\ \hline \end{array}$	4. $\begin{array}{r} 4 \\ \times\,6 \\ \hline \end{array}$	5. $\begin{array}{r} 9 \\ \times\,2 \\ \hline \end{array}$
6. $\begin{array}{r} 1 \\ \times\,5 \\ \hline \end{array}$	7. $\begin{array}{r} 6 \\ \times\,5 \\ \hline \end{array}$	8. $\begin{array}{r} 9 \\ \times\,5 \\ \hline \end{array}$	9. $\begin{array}{r} 9 \\ \times\,6 \\ \hline \end{array}$	10. $\begin{array}{r} 7 \\ \times\,3 \\ \hline \end{array}$
11. $\begin{array}{r} 5 \\ \times\,0 \\ \hline \end{array}$	12. $\begin{array}{r} 6 \\ \times\,0 \\ \hline \end{array}$	13. $\begin{array}{r} 8 \\ \times\,5 \\ \hline \end{array}$	14. $\begin{array}{r} 6 \\ \times\,7 \\ \hline \end{array}$	15. $\begin{array}{r} 5 \\ \times\,6 \\ \hline \end{array}$

16. $6 \times 6 =$	17. $5 \times 5 =$	18. $9 \times 5 =$	19. $3 \times 6 =$

Using Math

▷ Tom works in a supermarket. He put 5 boxes of juice on a shelf. Each box has 6 bottles. How many bottles did Tom put on the shelf?

Tom put _____ bottles on the shelf.

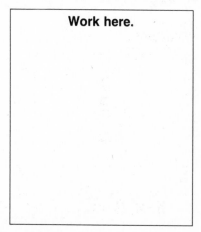

Work here.

Multiplying by 7

Study the multiplication table for 7 and memorize the facts.

×	0	1	2	3	4	5	6	7	8	9
7	0	7	14	21	28	35	42	49	56	63

How many dots are there?

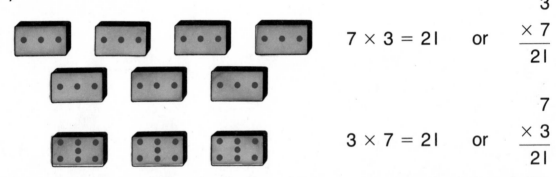

$7 \times 3 = 21$ or $\begin{array}{r} 3 \\ \times 7 \\ \hline 21 \end{array}$

$3 \times 7 = 21$ or $\begin{array}{r} 7 \\ \times 3 \\ \hline 21 \end{array}$

> **Remember that the order of the factors does not change the product.**
> $7 \times 3 = 21$ $3 \times 7 = 21$

Guided Practice

▷ Multiply.

1. $\begin{array}{r} 4 \\ \times 7 \\ \hline 28 \end{array}$	2. $\begin{array}{r} 6 \\ \times 7 \\ \hline \end{array}$	3. $\begin{array}{r} 7 \\ \times 6 \\ \hline \end{array}$	4. $\begin{array}{r} 9 \\ \times 7 \\ \hline \end{array}$
5. $7 \times 0 =$	6. $0 \times 7 =$	7. $2 \times 7 =$	8. $7 \times 8 =$

Practice

▷ Multiply.

1. $\begin{array}{r} 7 \\ \times\,3 \\ \hline \end{array}$	2. $\begin{array}{r} 7 \\ \times\,4 \\ \hline \end{array}$	3. $\begin{array}{r} 1 \\ \times\,7 \\ \hline \end{array}$	4. $\begin{array}{r} 3 \\ \times\,7 \\ \hline \end{array}$	5. $\begin{array}{r} 6 \\ \times\,5 \\ \hline \end{array}$
6. $\begin{array}{r} 9 \\ \times\,7 \\ \hline \end{array}$	7. $\begin{array}{r} 7 \\ \times\,6 \\ \hline \end{array}$	8. $\begin{array}{r} 7 \\ \times\,7 \\ \hline \end{array}$	9. $\begin{array}{r} 8 \\ \times\,4 \\ \hline \end{array}$	10. $\begin{array}{r} 7 \\ \times\,1 \\ \hline \end{array}$
11. $\begin{array}{r} 7 \\ \times\,8 \\ \hline \end{array}$	12. $\begin{array}{r} 7 \\ \times\,5 \\ \hline \end{array}$	13. $\begin{array}{r} 7 \\ \times\,9 \\ \hline \end{array}$	14. $\begin{array}{r} 7 \\ \times\,3 \\ \hline \end{array}$	15. $\begin{array}{r} 5 \\ \times\,7 \\ \hline \end{array}$

16. $7 \times 5 =$	17. $7 \times 8 =$	18. $7 \times 4 =$	19. $7 \times 2 =$

Using Math

▷ Rosa went to buy concert tickets. She waited in line. There were 7 lines. Each line had 6 people. How many people were in line?

There were _____ people in line.

Work here.

53

Multiplying by 8

The multiplication table for multiplying by 8 has only two new facts
for you to remember: $8 \times 8 = 64$ and $8 \times 9 = 72$

×	0	1	2	3	4	5	6	7	8	9
8	0	8	16	24	32	40	48	56	64	72

The order of multiplying eights does not change the answer.

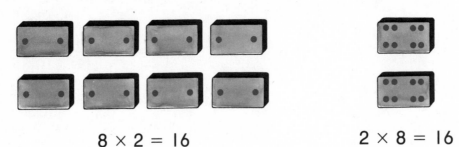

$$8 \times 2 = 16 \qquad\qquad 2 \times 8 = 16$$

Guided Practice

▷ Multiply.

1. $\begin{array}{r} 2 \\ \times\,8 \\ \hline 16 \end{array}$	2. $\begin{array}{r} 4 \\ \times\,8 \\ \hline \end{array}$	3. $\begin{array}{r} 8 \\ \times\,8 \\ \hline \end{array}$	4. $\begin{array}{r} 8 \\ \times\,5 \\ \hline \end{array}$
5. $8 \times 9 =$	6. $8 \times 6 =$	7. $8 \times 0 =$	8. $4 \times 8 =$

Practice

▷Multiply.

1. 8 × 8	2. 8 × 3	3. 8 × 1	4. 6 × 3	5. 9 × 8
6. 6 × 8	7. 8 × 6	8. 8 × 5	9. 1 × 8	10. 9 × 4
11. 8 × 2	12. 7 × 8	13. 5 × 8	14. 4 × 3	15. 8 × 6

16. 8 × 7 =	17. 8 × 2 =	18. 8 × 9 =	19. 8 × 3 =

Using Math

▷Kelly has a new puppy. The puppy is 8 weeks old.
How many days old is the puppy? (There are 7 days
in a week.)

The puppy is _____ days old.

Work here.

Multiplication Table 0–9

This multiplication table shows all the facts through 9. It can help you find the product of two factors.

×	0	1	2	3	4	5	6	7	8	9
0	0	0	0	0	0	0	0	0	0	0
1	0	1	2	3	4	5	6	7	8	9
2	0	2	4	6	8	10	12	14	16	18
3	0	3	6	9	12	15	18	21	24	27
4	0	4	8	12	16	20	24	28	32	36
5	0	5	10	15	20	25	30	35	40	45
6	0	6	12	18	24	30	36	42	48	54
7	0	7	14	21	28	35	42	49	56	63
8	0	8	16	24	32	40	48	56	64	72
9	0	9	18	27	36	45	54	63	72	81

This is how you use the table to find the product of 9 × 9.

Step 1 Find the first factor in the column under the ×.

Step 2 Move to the right until you are under the second factor.

Step 3 Read the product: 81.

Guided Practice

▷Find each product using the multiplication table above.

1. $8 \times 8 = 64$	2. $6 \times 6 =$	3. $4 \times 9 =$	4. $2 \times 6 =$
5. $7 \times 7 =$	6. $9 \times 8 =$	7. $8 \times 5 =$	8. $3 \times 5 =$

56

Practice

▷ Multiply. You may use the multiplication table.

1. 5 7 × 7 × 5	**2.** 8 6 × 6 × 8	**3.** 9 5 × 5 × 9
4. 7 4 × 4 × 7	**5.** 6 7 × 7 × 6	**6.** 9 8 × 8 × 9
7. 8 4 × 4 × 8	**8.** 8 3 × 3 × 8	**9.** 7 9 × 9 × 7
10. 6 × 2 = 2 × 6 =	**11.** 7 × 8 = 8 × 7 =	**12.** 9 × 6 = 6 × 9 =

Using Math

▷ Tony has a paper route. He has 9 apartment houses on his route. He leaves 6 papers in each apartment house. How many papers does he leave in all?

He leaves _____ papers.

Work here.

Time Before the Hour

You can say the time is 5:47 or 47 minutes after 5. You can also read this time by counting the minute marks before or **to the hour.**

What time is it?

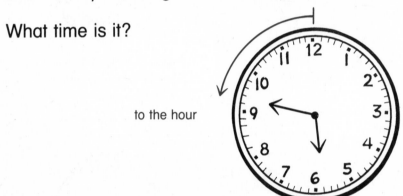

to the hour

| Step 1 | Look at the minute hand. Start at the 12. Count by fives to the number just before the minute hand (5-10). Then count by ones (10-11-12-13). |

| Step 2 | Look at the hour hand. It is between 5 and 6. When you count **to the hour,** the larger number is the hour. The hour is 6. |

The time is 13 minutes to 6.

Guided Practice

▷Write each time two ways.

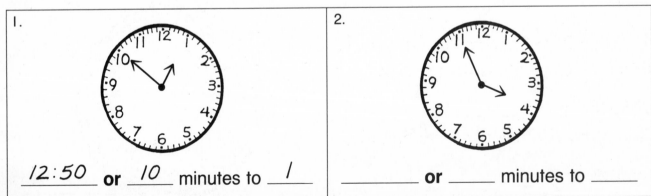

| 1. |
| 12:50 or 10 minutes to 1 |

| 2. |
| _____ or ____ minutes to _____ |

Practice

▷ Write each time two ways.

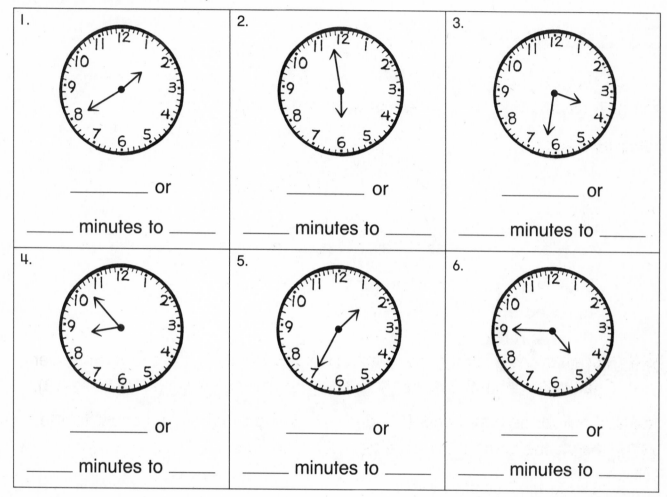

1.

_____ or

_____ minutes to _____

2.

_____ or

_____ minutes to _____

3.

_____ or

_____ minutes to _____

4.

_____ or

_____ minutes to _____

5.

_____ or

_____ minutes to _____

6.

_____ or

_____ minutes to _____

Using Math

▷ The train from Concord will arrive at 10:00.
Read the clock at the train station.

Write the time. _____
How many minutes are there before

the train arrives? _____ minutes

Problem Solving

Estimation

Jorge threw a ball 39 feet.
He wanted to know if that is nearer to 30 or 40 feet.

Step 1 ▶ Draw a number line that shows the nearest ten
below and above 39.

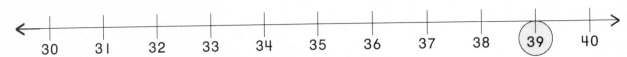

Step 2 ▶ Look at 39 on the number line.
Is it nearer to 30 or 40?
It is nearer to <u>40</u>.

Jorge threw the ball **about** 40 feet.

> The word *about* means an exact answer is not needed.
> You can estimate the answer.

Guided Practice

▶ Round to the nearest ten.

1. Megan threw a ball 24 feet.
Is that nearer to 20 or 30?

   It is nearer to <u>20</u>.

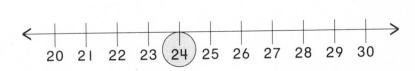

2. Chi kicked a football 43 feet.
Is that nearer to 40 or 50?

   It is nearer to _____.

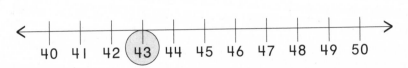

Practice

▷ Round to the nearest ten.

1. Ana has 24 shells.
   Is that nearer to 20 or 30?

   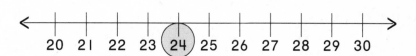

   It is nearer to _____.

2. Island School has 76 students.
   Is that nearer to 70 or 80?

   It is nearer to _____.

3. Tom sold 63 tickets.
   Is that nearer to 60 or 70?

   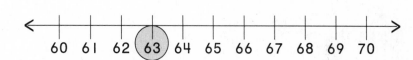

   It is nearer to _____.

4. Mario drove 96 miles.
   Is that nearer to 90 or 100?

   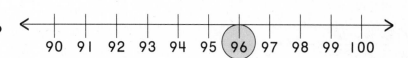

   It is nearer to _____.

5. There are 87 people at the game.
   Is that nearer to 80 or 90?

   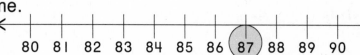

   It is nearer to _____.

▶Multiply.

pages 46–47 1. **6** **× 0**	2. **8** **× 1**	3. **4** **× 2**	4. **2** **× 1**
pages 48–49 5. **4** **× 3**	6. **5** **× 4**	7. **6** **× 3**	8. **7** **× 4**
pages 50–51 9. **7** **× 5**	10. **9** **× 6**	11. **3** **× 5**	12. **8** **× 6**
13. **6** **× 5**	14. **7** **× 6**	15. **4** **× 5**	16. **6** **× 6**
pages 52–53 17. **2** **× 7**	18. **0** **× 7**	19. **6** **× 7**	20. **4** **× 7**
21. **1** **× 7**	22. **8** **× 7**	23. **3** **× 7**	24. **9** **× 7**

▷Multiply.

pages 54–55			
25. $\begin{array}{r} 2 \\ \times\ 8 \\ \hline \end{array}$	26. $\begin{array}{r} 5 \\ \times\ 8 \\ \hline \end{array}$	27. $\begin{array}{r} 7 \\ \times\ 8 \\ \hline \end{array}$	28. $\begin{array}{r} 9 \\ \times\ 8 \\ \hline \end{array}$
29. $\begin{array}{r} 3 \\ \times\ 8 \\ \hline \end{array}$	30. $\begin{array}{r} 6 \\ \times\ 8 \\ \hline \end{array}$	31. $\begin{array}{r} 4 \\ \times\ 8 \\ \hline \end{array}$	32. $\begin{array}{r} 8 \\ \times\ 8 \\ \hline \end{array}$
pages 56–57			
33. $\begin{array}{r} 0 \\ \times\ 9 \\ \hline \end{array}$	34. $\begin{array}{r} 6 \\ \times\ 9 \\ \hline \end{array}$	35. $\begin{array}{r} 9 \\ \times\ 9 \\ \hline \end{array}$	36. $\begin{array}{r} 3 \\ \times\ 9 \\ \hline \end{array}$
37. $\begin{array}{r} 7 \\ \times\ 9 \\ \hline \end{array}$	38. $\begin{array}{r} 1 \\ \times\ 9 \\ \hline \end{array}$	39. $\begin{array}{r} 8 \\ \times\ 9 \\ \hline \end{array}$	40. $\begin{array}{r} 5 \\ \times\ 9 \\ \hline \end{array}$

▷Write each time two ways.   pages 58–59

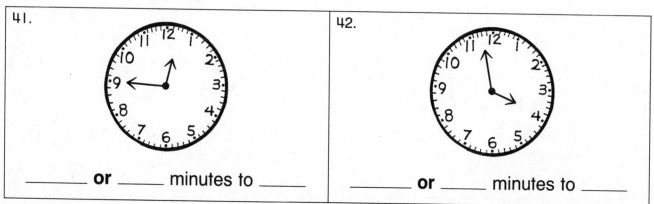

41. _____ **or** _____ minutes to _____

42. _____ **or** _____ minutes to _____

▶Round to the nearest ten.
pages 60–61

43. Alvin has 27 doughnuts.
    Is that nearer to 20 or 30?

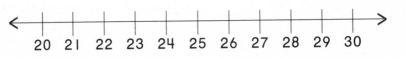

    It is nearer to _____.

_____

44. Pam kicked a ball 64 feet.
    Is that nearer to 60 or 70?

    It is nearer to _____.

_____

45. Charlie has 59 baseball cards.
    Is that nearer to 50 or 60?

    It is nearer to _____.

_____

46. Chi painted 12 pictures.
    Is that nearer to 10 or 20?

    It is nearer to _____.

_____

47. Anne drove her car 86 miles.
    Is that nearer to 80 or 90?

    It is nearer to _____.

▷ Multiply.

1. $\begin{array}{r} 7 \\ \times\ 0 \\ \hline \end{array}$	2. $\begin{array}{r} 6 \\ \times\ 2 \\ \hline \end{array}$	3. $\begin{array}{r} 8 \\ \times\ 4 \\ \hline \end{array}$	4. $\begin{array}{r} 5 \\ \times\ 3 \\ \hline \end{array}$
5. $\begin{array}{r} 8 \\ \times\ 5 \\ \hline \end{array}$	6. $\begin{array}{r} 4 \\ \times\ 6 \\ \hline \end{array}$	7. $\begin{array}{r} 1 \\ \times\ 6 \\ \hline \end{array}$	8. $\begin{array}{r} 9 \\ \times\ 5 \\ \hline \end{array}$
9. $\begin{array}{r} 6 \\ \times\ 7 \\ \hline \end{array}$	10. $\begin{array}{r} 3 \\ \times\ 9 \\ \hline \end{array}$	11. $\begin{array}{r} 6 \\ \times\ 8 \\ \hline \end{array}$	12. $\begin{array}{r} 7 \\ \times\ 9 \\ \hline \end{array}$
13. $\begin{array}{r} 7 \\ \times\ 8 \\ \hline \end{array}$	14. $\begin{array}{r} 5 \\ \times\ 7 \\ \hline \end{array}$	15. $\begin{array}{r} 8 \\ \times\ 9 \\ \hline \end{array}$	16. $\begin{array}{r} 7 \\ \times\ 7 \\ \hline \end{array}$

▷ Write each time two ways.

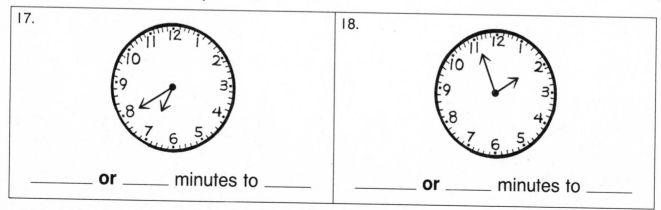

17. _____ **or** _____ minutes to _____

18. _____ **or** _____ minutes to _____

▷Round to the nearest ten.

19. 87 people watched a ball game.
    Is that nearer to 80 or 90?

It is nearer to _____.

_____

20. Paula sold 42 drinks at the game.
    Is that nearer to 40 or 50?

It is nearer to _____.

_____

21. Amy hit a baseball 74 feet.
    Is that nearer to 70 or 80?

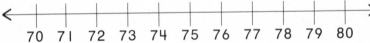

It is nearer to _____.

_____

22. 24 people bought team pennants.
    Is that nearer to 20 or 30?

It is nearer to _____.

_____

23. Casey ran 18 feet to catch a ball.
    Is that nearer to 10 or 20?

It is nearer to _____.

Cumulative Review

▷ Write each missing number.   pages 2–3

1. 65 = _____ tens _____ ones

2. 46 = _____ tens _____ ones

3. 79 = _____ tens _____ ones

4. 33 = _____ tens _____ ones

5. 628 = _____ hundreds _____ tens _____ ones

6. 555 = _____ hundreds _____ tens _____ ones

▷ Write each number in standard form.   pages 4–5

7. 4,000 + 800 + 50 + 2 = _____

8. 1,000 + 200 + 30 + 9 = _____

9. 7,000 + 600 + 90 + 4 = _____

10. 5,000 + 400 + 50 = _____

▷ Write the value of each underlined digit.   pages 6–7

11. 42,713 _____

12. 12,674 _____

13. 19,891 _____

14. 73,876 _____

15. 10,204 _____

16. 25,563 _____

▷ Compare. Ring > or <.   pages 8–9

17. 146 $\overset{>}{\underset{<}{}}$ 164	18. 852 $\overset{>}{\underset{<}{}}$ 851	19. 1,516 $\overset{>}{\underset{<}{}}$ 1,420
20. 32,120 $\overset{>}{\underset{<}{}}$ 32,133	21. 6,909 $\overset{>}{\underset{<}{}}$ 6,919	22. 544 $\overset{>}{\underset{<}{}}$ 549

▷Round each number to the nearest ten. pages 10–11

23. 19 _____   24. 32 _____   25. 73 _____

26. 86 _____   27. 55 _____   28. 26 _____

▷Round each number to the nearest ten. pages 12–13

29. 437 _____   30. 253 _____   31. 3,318 _____

32. 2,245 _____   33. 8,242 _____   34. 623 _____

▷Round each number to the nearest hundred. pages 12–13

35. 276 _____   36. 145 _____   37. 42,281 _____

38. 640 _____   39. 3,456 _____   40. 523 _____

▷Round each number to the nearest thousand. pages 12–13

41. 1,386 _____   42. 3,792 _____   43. 26,113 _____

44. 6,500 _____   45. 43,240 _____   46. 55,696 _____

▷Write each time. pages 14–15

47.	48.	49.
		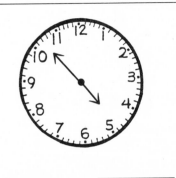
_____	_____	_____

A lifeguard made this graph to show how many people are using the pool each day it is open.

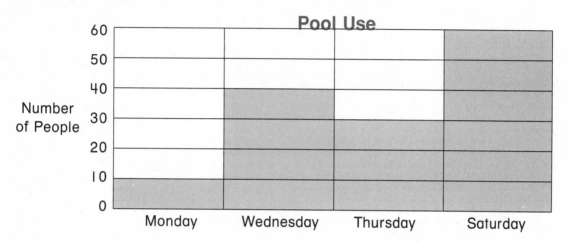

▷Look at the graph.

Write how many people used the pool.
pages 16–17

50. _____ people on Wednesday	51. _____ people on Thursday

▷Use the graph to answer.

52. What day is the pool used most? _____	53. What day is the pool used least? _____
54. How many more people used the pool on Wednesday than on Monday? _____ more people	55. How many more people used the pool on Saturday than on Thursday? _____ more people

CHAPTER 2

Cumulative Review

▷Add.

pages 24–25 1. 7 + 4	2. 6 + 3	3. 9 + 6	4. 5 + 8
pages 26–27 5. 42 + 17	6. 63 + 36	7. 25 + 73	8. 37 + 34
9. 56 + 27	10. 75 + 15	11. 39 + 22	12. 47 + 48
pages 28–29 13. 573 + 218	14. 666 + 141	15. 487 + 466	16. 493 + 168
17. 342 + 179	18. 6,496 + 508	19. 2,468 + 1,701	20. 7,692 + 1,310

▷Subtract.

pages 30–31 21. 11 − 7	22. 10 − 5	23. 13 − 6	24. 17 − 8

▷ Subtract.

pages 32–33

25. $\quad 76$ $\quad -51$	26. $\quad 89$ $\quad -34$	27. $\quad 52$ $\quad -35$	28. $\quad 91$ $\quad -64$
29. $\quad 42$ $\quad -14$	30. $\quad 46$ $\quad -27$	31. $\quad 63$ $\quad -38$	32. $\quad 37$ $\quad -19$

pages 34–35

33. $\quad 629$ $\quad -103$	34. $\quad 876$ $\quad -438$	35. $\quad 592$ $\quad -162$	36. $\quad 726$ $\quad -457$
37. $\quad 423$ $\quad -189$	38. $\quad 1,592$ $\quad -\;\;\;493$	39. $\quad 3,765$ $\quad -1,842$	40. $\quad 8,347$ $\quad -3,682$

▷ Write each time two ways. pages 36–37

41.	42.
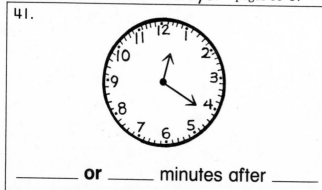	
_____ **or** _____ minutes after _____	_____ **or** _____ minutes after _____

▷ Use each table to make a graph.

pages 38–39

43. Adams' Sports made this table to show how many mountain bikes they sold in 4 months.

Bike Sales	
May	6
June	8
July	2
August	4

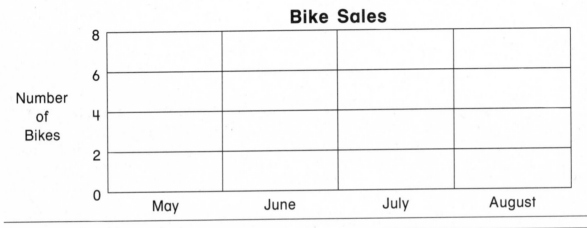

Bike Sales

44. Diaz's Sports made this table to show how many pairs of skates they sold in 4 months.

Skate Sales	
May	20
June	30
July	20
August	40

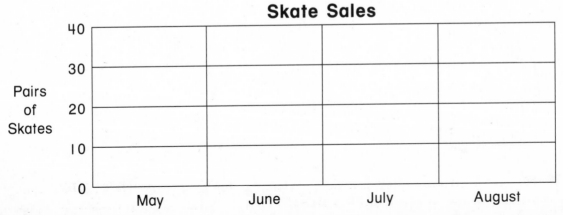

Skate Sales

▷ Multiply.

pages 46–49			
1. $\begin{array}{r} 7 \\ \times\ 3 \\ \hline \end{array}$	2. $\begin{array}{r} 7 \\ \times\ 1 \\ \hline \end{array}$	3. $\begin{array}{r} 6 \\ \times\ 2 \\ \hline \end{array}$	4. $\begin{array}{r} 9 \\ \times\ 4 \\ \hline \end{array}$
pages 50–51			
5. $\begin{array}{r} 3 \\ \times\ 5 \\ \hline \end{array}$	6. $\begin{array}{r} 5 \\ \times\ 6 \\ \hline \end{array}$	7. $\begin{array}{r} 8 \\ \times\ 5 \\ \hline \end{array}$	8. $\begin{array}{r} 7 \\ \times\ 6 \\ \hline \end{array}$
pages 52–57			
9. $\begin{array}{r} 1 \\ \times\ 7 \\ \hline \end{array}$	10. $\begin{array}{r} 2 \\ \times\ 8 \\ \hline \end{array}$	11. $\begin{array}{r} 6 \\ \times\ 9 \\ \hline \end{array}$	12. $\begin{array}{r} 7 \\ \times\ 7 \\ \hline \end{array}$
13. $\begin{array}{r} 4 \\ \times\ 8 \\ \hline \end{array}$	14. $\begin{array}{r} 6 \\ \times\ 7 \\ \hline \end{array}$	15. $\begin{array}{r} 6 \\ \times\ 8 \\ \hline \end{array}$	16. $\begin{array}{r} 9 \\ \times\ 9 \\ \hline \end{array}$

▷ Write each time two ways.   pages 58–59

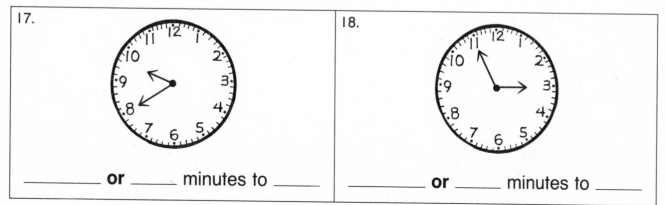

17. _____ **or** _____ minutes to _____

18. _____ **or** _____ minutes to _____

▷ Round to the nearest ten.
pages 60–61

19. Stan drove 19 miles to the store.
Is that nearer to 10 or 20?

10 11 12 13 14 15 16 17 18 19 20

It is nearer to _____.

20. Pearl put 56 cans on a shelf.
Is that nearer to 50 or 60?

50 51 52 53 54 55 56 57 58 59 60

It is nearer to _____.

21. 84 people shopped in the store on Monday.
Is that nearer to 80 or 90?

80 81 82 83 84 85 86 87 88 89 90

It is nearer to _____.

22. Sean bagged 96 sacks of groceries.
Is that nearer to 90 or 100?

90 91 92 93 94 95 96 97 98 99 100

It is nearer to _____.

23. Cally put 44 apples in a bin.
Is that nearer to 40 or 50?

40 41 42 43 44 45 46 47 48 49 50

It is nearer to _____.

Multiplying by 1-Digit Numbers

▼ ▼ ▼ ▼ ▼ ▼ ▼

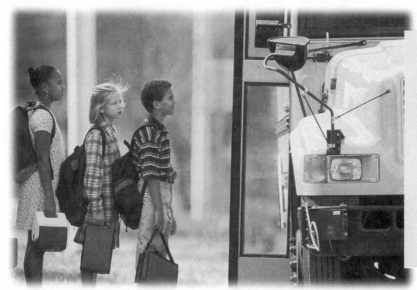

Carlo and his friends rode to school on a bus that had 11 bench seats on each side. How many bench seats in all were on their school bus? If 2 people sat on each bench, how many passengers were on the bus?

Solve.

▷ Write a problem about the way that you get to school.

Tens, Hundreds, and Thousands

You can use the multiplication facts through 9 to multiply large numbers.

Multiplication fact	Multiply 4 tens by 2.
$\begin{array}{r} 4 \\ \times\ 2 \\ \hline 8 \end{array}$	$\begin{array}{r} 4 \text{ tens} \\ \times\ 2 \\ \hline 8 \text{ tens} \end{array}$ $\quad$ $\begin{array}{r} 4 \text{ tens} = 40 \\ \times\ 2 \\ \hline 8 \text{ tens} = 80 \end{array}$

Multiply 4 hundreds by 2.	Multiply 4 thousands by 2.
$\begin{array}{r} 4 \text{ hundreds} \\ \times\ 2 \\ \hline 8 \text{ hundreds} \end{array}$ $\quad$ $\begin{array}{r} 4 \text{ hundreds} = 400 \\ \times\ 2 \\ \hline 8 \text{ hundreds} = 800 \end{array}$	$\begin{array}{r} 4 \text{ thousands} \\ \times\ 2 \\ \hline 8 \text{ thousands} \end{array}$ $\quad$ $\begin{array}{r} 4 \text{ thousands} = 4{,}000 \\ \times\ 2 \\ \hline 8 \text{ thousands} = 8{,}000 \end{array}$

Look at the zero pattern. What do you see?

$\begin{array}{r} 6 \\ \times\ 3 \\ \hline 18 \end{array}$	$\begin{array}{r} 60 \\ \times\ 3 \\ \hline 180 \end{array}$	$\begin{array}{r} 600 \\ \times\ 3 \\ \hline 1{,}800 \end{array}$	$\begin{array}{r} 6{,}000 \\ \times\ 3 \\ \hline 18{,}000 \end{array}$		$\begin{array}{r} 6 \\ \times\ 4 \\ \hline 24 \end{array}$	$\begin{array}{r} 60 \\ \times\ 4 \\ \hline 240 \end{array}$	$\begin{array}{r} 600 \\ \times\ 4 \\ \hline 2{,}400 \end{array}$	$\begin{array}{r} 6{,}000 \\ \times\ 4 \\ \hline 24{,}000 \end{array}$

Guided Practice

▷ Multiply.

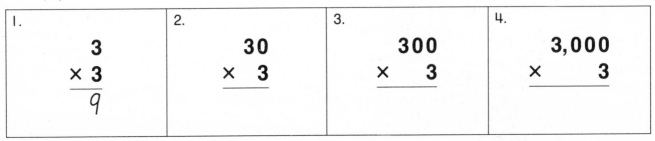

1.	2.	3.	4.
$\begin{array}{r} 3 \\ \times\ 3 \\ \hline 9 \end{array}$	$\begin{array}{r} 30 \\ \times\ 3 \\ \hline \end{array}$	$\begin{array}{r} 300 \\ \times\ 3 \\ \hline \end{array}$	$\begin{array}{r} 3{,}000 \\ \times\ 3 \\ \hline \end{array}$

Practice

▷Multiply.

1. $\begin{array}{r} 2 \\ \times\ 2 \\ \hline \end{array}$	2. $\begin{array}{r} 20 \\ \times\ 2 \\ \hline \end{array}$	3. $\begin{array}{r} 10 \\ \times\ 3 \\ \hline \end{array}$	4. $\begin{array}{r} 100 \\ \times\ \ 3 \\ \hline \end{array}$	5. $\begin{array}{r} 300 \\ \times\ \ 4 \\ \hline \end{array}$
6. $\begin{array}{r} 3,000 \\ \times\ \ \ \ 4 \\ \hline \end{array}$	7. $\begin{array}{r} 40 \\ \times\ 2 \\ \hline \end{array}$	8. $\begin{array}{r} 400 \\ \times\ \ 2 \\ \hline \end{array}$	9. $\begin{array}{r} 60 \\ \times\ 3 \\ \hline \end{array}$	10. $\begin{array}{r} 600 \\ \times\ \ 3 \\ \hline \end{array}$
11. $\begin{array}{r} 6,000 \\ \times\ \ \ \ 3 \\ \hline \end{array}$	12. $\begin{array}{r} 50 \\ \times\ 3 \\ \hline \end{array}$	13. $\begin{array}{r} 20 \\ \times\ 8 \\ \hline \end{array}$	14. $\begin{array}{r} 200 \\ \times\ \ 8 \\ \hline \end{array}$	15. $\begin{array}{r} 2,000 \\ \times\ \ \ \ 8 \\ \hline \end{array}$

Using Math

▷Mary bought 2 sacks of dog food. Each sack holds 50 pounds. How many pounds did she buy in all?

She bought _____ pounds of dog food.

Work here.

77

Multiplying Ones and Tens

Each school bus carries 24 students. How many students are on both buses?

Multiply 2 × 24 to find the answer.

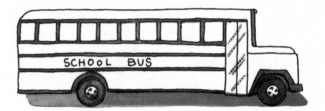

Step 1 ▶ Multiply the 4 ones by 2.

tens	ones
2	4
×	2
	8

Step 2 ▶ Multiply the 2 tens by 2.

tens	ones
2	4
×	2
4	8

There are 48 students on the two buses.

Guided Practice

▶ Multiply.

1.	2.	3.	4.	5.
34 × 2 — 68	42 × 2	13 × 3	11 × 7	40 × 2

78

Practice

▷ Multiply.

1. $\begin{array}{r} 11 \\ \times\ 9 \\ \hline \end{array}$	2. $\begin{array}{r} 22 \\ \times\ 2 \\ \hline \end{array}$	3. $\begin{array}{r} 30 \\ \times\ 3 \\ \hline \end{array}$	4. $\begin{array}{r} 12 \\ \times\ 4 \\ \hline \end{array}$	5. $\begin{array}{r} 11 \\ \times\ 5 \\ \hline \end{array}$
6. $\begin{array}{r} 44 \\ \times\ 2 \\ \hline \end{array}$	7. $\begin{array}{r} 20 \\ \times\ 4 \\ \hline \end{array}$	8. $\begin{array}{r} 13 \\ \times\ 2 \\ \hline \end{array}$	9. $\begin{array}{r} 42 \\ \times\ 2 \\ \hline \end{array}$	10. $\begin{array}{r} 12 \\ \times\ 2 \\ \hline \end{array}$
11. $\begin{array}{r} 13 \\ \times\ 3 \\ \hline \end{array}$	12. $\begin{array}{r} 21 \\ \times\ 4 \\ \hline \end{array}$	13. $\begin{array}{r} 10 \\ \times\ 8 \\ \hline \end{array}$	14. $\begin{array}{r} 14 \\ \times\ 2 \\ \hline \end{array}$	15. $\begin{array}{r} 10 \\ \times\ 6 \\ \hline \end{array}$

Using Math

▷ There are 3 boxes of new books for the library. Each box holds 12 books. How many new books are there in all?

There are _____ new books in all.

Work here.

79

Multiplication with Regrouping

Sarah is in charge of the balloon-throwing contest for the carnival. She bought 8 dozen balloons. How many balloons did she buy?

Multiply 8 × 12 to find the answer.

Step 1 Multiply the 2 ones by 8.

8 × 2 ones = 16 ones

Regroup 16 ones as 1 ten 6 ones.

Write 6 in the ones' place.

Write 1 in the tens' column.

tens	ones
1	
1	2
×	8
	6

Step 2 Multiply the 1 ten by 8.

8 × 1 ten = 8 tens

Then add the 1 ten.

8 tens + 1 ten = 9 tens

Write 9 in the tens' place.

tens	ones
1	
1	2
×	8
9	6

Guided Practice

▶Multiply.

1.	2.	3.	4.	5.
1 19 × 2 —— 38	13 × 3	16 × 4	19 × 3	12 × 5

80

Practice

▷ Multiply.

1. 24 × 3	2. 12 × 7	3. 12 × 3	4. 12 × 5	5. 17 × 2
6. 15 × 6	7. 14 × 4	8. 23 × 4	9. 16 × 2	10. 19 × 3
11. 16 × 3	12. 12 × 4	13. 17 × 4	14. 19 × 4	15. 17 × 5

Using Math

▷ James works in a building that has 6 flights of stairs.
Each flight has 16 steps. How many steps does
James have to climb to get to the top floor?

He has to climb _____ steps.

Work here.

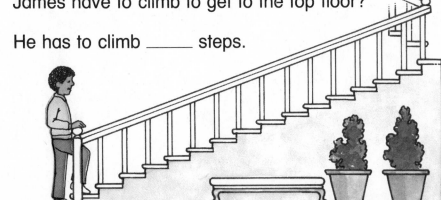

81

Multiplication with Regrouping

Sometimes when you multiply, the answer is greater than 100.
How many stars are there?

★ ★ ★ ★ ★ ★ ★ ★ ★ ★ ★ ★   ★ ★ ★ ★ ★ ★ ★ ★ ★ ★ ★ ★   ★ ★ ★ ★ ★ ★ ★ ★ ★ ★ ★ ★
★ ★ ★ ★ ★ ★ ★ ★ ★ ★ ★ ★   ★ ★ ★ ★ ★ ★ ★ ★ ★ ★ ★ ★   ★ ★ ★ ★ ★ ★ ★ ★ ★ ★ ★ ★
★ ★ ★ ★ ★ ★ ★ ★ ★ ★ ★ ★   ★ ★ ★ ★ ★ ★ ★ ★ ★ ★ ★ ★   ★ ★ ★ ★ ★ ★ ★ ★ ★ ★ ★ ★
★ ★ ★ ★ ★ ★ ★ ★ ★ ★ ★ ★   ★ ★ ★ ★ ★ ★ ★ ★ ★ ★ ★ ★   ★ ★ ★ ★ ★ ★ ★ ★ ★ ★ ★ ★

Multiply 3×48.

Step 1 Multiply the 8 ones by 3.

3×8 ones = 24 ones

Regroup 24 ones as 2 tens 4 ones.

Write 4 in the ones' place.

Write 2 in the tens' column.

$$\begin{array}{r} 2 \\ 48 \\ \times\,3 \\ \hline 4 \end{array}$$

Step 2 Multiply the 4 tens by 3.

3×4 tens = 12 tens

Add the 2 tens.

12 tens + 2 tens = 14 tens

Regroup 14 tens as 1 hundred 4 tens.

Write 4 in the tens' place.

Write 1 in the hundreds' place.

$$\begin{array}{r} 2 \\ 48 \\ \times\,3 \\ \hline 144 \end{array}$$

Guided Practice

▷ Multiply.

1. $\begin{array}{r} {\scriptstyle 1} \\ 52 \\ \times\,6 \\ \hline 312 \end{array}$	2. $\begin{array}{r} 47 \\ \times\,4 \\ \hline \end{array}$	3. $\begin{array}{r} 33 \\ \times\,6 \\ \hline \end{array}$	4. $\begin{array}{r} 27 \\ \times\,8 \\ \hline \end{array}$	5. $\begin{array}{r} 42 \\ \times\,4 \\ \hline \end{array}$

Practice

Multiply.

1.	2.	3.	4.	5.
23 × 6	55 × 4	17 × 9	31 × 4	52 × 2
6.	7.	8.	9.	10.
21 × 7	27 × 6	92 × 3	85 × 3	57 × 2
11.	12.	13.	14.	15.
19 × 8	24 × 8	41 × 4	77 × 6	13 × 7

Problem Solving

There are 34 rows of seats in the new movie theater.
Is that nearer to 30 or 40?

It is nearer to _____ .

Multiplying Larger Numbers

A movie theater holds 175 people. Three shows are given on Saturday. How many people can see the movie on Saturday?

Step 1 ▶ Multiply the 5 ones by 3.

3×5 ones $= 15$ ones

Regroup 15 ones as 1 ten 5 ones.

Write 5 in the ones' place.

Write 1 in the tens' column.

$$
\begin{array}{r}
1 \\
175 \\
\times\quad 3 \\
\hline
5
\end{array}
$$

Step 2 ▶ Multiply the 7 tens by 3.

3×7 tens $= 21$ tens

Add 1 ten to get 22 tens.

Regroup 22 tens as 2 hundreds 2 tens.

Write 2 in the tens' place.

Write 2 in the hundreds' column.

$$
\begin{array}{r}
2\ 1 \\
175 \\
\times\quad 3 \\
\hline
25
\end{array}
$$

Step 3 ▶ Multiply the 1 hundred by 3.

3×1 hundred $= 3$ hundreds

Add the 2 hundreds to get 5 hundreds.

Write 5 in the hundreds' place.

$$
\begin{array}{r}
2\ 1 \\
175 \\
\times\quad 3 \\
\hline
525
\end{array}
$$

Guided Practice

▷ Multiply.

1.	2.	3.	4.	5.
$\begin{array}{r} 1\ 3 \\ 127 \\ \times\ \ 5 \\ \hline 635 \end{array}$	$\begin{array}{r} 155 \\ \times\ \ 4 \\ \hline \end{array}$	$\begin{array}{r} 312 \\ \times\ \ 3 \\ \hline \end{array}$	$\begin{array}{r} 244 \\ \times\ \ 3 \\ \hline \end{array}$	$\begin{array}{r} 123 \\ \times\ \ 8 \\ \hline \end{array}$

Practice

▷ Multiply.

1. 234 × 3	2. 415 × 2	3. 122 × 4	4. 135 × 6	5. 121 × 5
6. 304 × 2	7. 245 × 3	8. 142 × 5	9. 157 × 4	10. 417 × 2
11. 114 × 3	12. 242 × 3	13. 352 × 2	14. 112 × 5	15. 176 × 2

Using Math

▷ The new movie theater holds 162 people. There will be 3 shows on Sunday. Suppose each person buys a box of popcorn. How many boxes of popcorn will be sold?

_____ boxes of popcorn will be sold.

Work here.

Larger Products

When you multiply 432 by 4, the answer is greater than 1,000.

Step 1 ▶ Multiply the ones.

$4 \times 2 = 8$

Write 8 in the ones' place.

$$\begin{array}{r} 432 \\ \times\quad 4 \\ \hline 8 \end{array}$$

Step 2 ▶ Multiply the tens.

4×3 tens $= 12$ tens

Regroup 12 tens as 1 hundred 2 tens.

Write 2 in the tens' place.

Write 1 in the hundreds' column.

$$\begin{array}{r} 1 \\ 432 \\ \times\quad 4 \\ \hline 28 \end{array}$$

Step 3 ▶ Multiply the hundreds.

4×4 hundreds $= 16$ hundreds

Add 1 hundred to get 17 hundreds.

Regroup 17 hundreds as 1 thousand 7 hundreds.

Write 7 in the hundreds' place.

Write 1 in the thousands' place.

$$\begin{array}{r} 1 \\ 432 \\ \times\quad 4 \\ \hline 1,728 \end{array}$$

Guided Practice

▶ Multiply.

1.	2.	3.	4.	5.
$\begin{array}{r} 1 \\ 421 \\ \times\quad 5 \\ \hline 2,105 \end{array}$	$\begin{array}{r} 573 \\ \times\quad 2 \\ \hline \end{array}$	$\begin{array}{r} 642 \\ \times\quad 3 \\ \hline \end{array}$	$\begin{array}{r} 874 \\ \times\quad 3 \\ \hline \end{array}$	$\begin{array}{r} 362 \\ \times\quad 4 \\ \hline \end{array}$

Practice

▷ Multiply.

1.
 	
   245
×   6
	2.
	
	   376
	× 3
		3.
		
		   504
		× 2
			4.
			
			   617
			× 5
				5.
				
				   392
				× 4

6.
 	
   493
×   8
	7.
	
	   812
	× 4
		8.
		
		   777
		× 5
			9.
			
			   129
			× 8
				10.
				
				   656
				× 7

11.
 	
   669
×   8
	12.
	
	   285
	× 9
		13.
		
		   404
		× 7
			14.
			
			   839
			× 9
				15.
				
				   318
				× 8

Using Math

▷ Three jets took off for New York City. Each jet had 376 people on board. How many people were on the jets?

There were _____ people on the jets.

Work here.

A.M. and P.M.

A day begins at 12:00 at night. It is called **midnight.** The 12 hours from midnight to 12:00 are **A.M.** hours.

The second 12:00 is called **noon.** The 12 hours from noon to midnight are called **P.M.** hours.

| 12:00 midnight | 1 | 2 | 3 | 4 | 5 | 6 | 7 | 8 | 9 | 10 | 11 | 12:00 noon | 1 | 2 | 3 | 4 | 5 | 6 | 7 | 8 | 9 | 10 | 11 | 12:00 midnight |

A.M.   P.M.

Guided Practice

▷Ring A.M. or P.M.

1. Pam goes to bed at 9:30.   A.M.   (P.M.)

2. Rodney eats lunch at 1:00.   A.M.   P.M.

3. Sarah leaves school at 3:30.   A.M.   P.M.

4. Jason eats breakfast at 7:05.   A.M.   P.M.

5. Carmen wakes up at 6:30.   A.M.   P.M.

Practice

▷ Ring A.M. or P.M.

1. Grace eats breakfast at 7:30.   A.M.   P.M.

2. Dale goes to dance class at 4:30.   A.M.   P.M.

3. Jack gets dressed at 7:15.   A.M.   P.M.

4. Joan eats lunch at 12:30.   A.M.   P.M.

5. Diane wakes up at 7:00.   A.M.   P.M.

6. Ann goes to bed at 9:00.   A.M.   P.M.

7. Bob plays baseball at 3:30.   A.M.   P.M.

8. Craig leaves school at 4:00.   A.M.   P.M.

9. George goes to school at 7:45.   A.M.   P.M.

10. Kathy takes a nap at 1:30.   A.M.   P.M.

11. Ryan's class has recess at 11:00.   A.M.   P.M.

12. Pat plays soccer at 4:00.   A.M.   P.M.

Using Math

▷ The time is now 7:30 A.M. Saul has tickets to go to the baseball game. The game starts at 7:00 P.M. Check (√) each box that tells something Saul can do between now and the time the game starts.

☐ Eat breakfast at 7:00 A.M.   ☐ Do homework at 3:30 P.M.

☐ Sweep the garage at 5:00 P.M.   ☐ Watch T.V. at 8:00 P.M.

Problem Solving

Estimation

Each bus has 41 students on it. There are 6 buses.
About how many students in all are there?

> The word **about** means an exact answer is not needed.
> You can **estimate** the answer.

Round to the nearest ten.

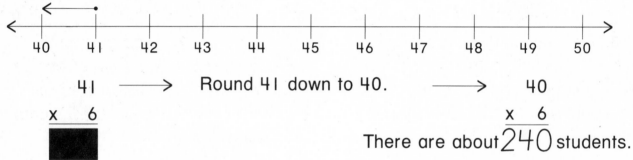

41 $\longrightarrow$ Round 41 down to 40. $\longrightarrow$ 40

$$\begin{array}{r} 41 \\ \times\ 6 \\ \hline \blacksquare \end{array}$$

$$\begin{array}{r} 40 \\ \times\ 6 \\ \hline \end{array}$$ There are about 240 students.

Guided Practice

▷ Round to the nearest ten.
Estimate to solve.

1. Terri set up 96 chairs in front of the stage.
   About how many people can see the play
   in 3 show times?

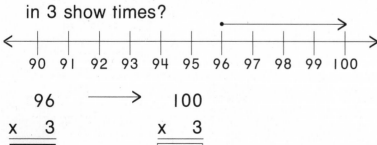

96 $\longrightarrow$ 100

$$\begin{array}{r} \times\ 3 \\ \hline \blacksquare \end{array}$$

$$\begin{array}{r} \times\ 3 \\ \hline \end{array}$$ about ☐ people

Practice

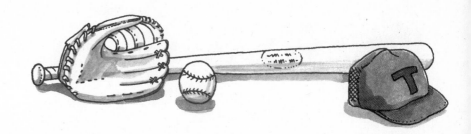

Round to the nearest ten.
Estimate to solve.

---

1. Hermie's class has 23 students.
   Each student has 6 books.
   About how many books in all
   are there?

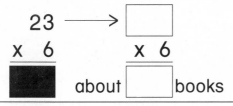

about _____ books

2. Alita needed 8 strips of ribbon.
   Each strip must be 38 inches.
   About how many inches of
   ribbon will Alita need?

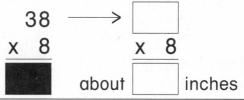

about _____ inches

---

3. A can of coffee weighed
   2 pounds. A store bought a
   case of 24 cans. About how
   much does the case of coffee
   weigh?

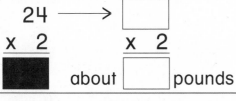

about _____ pounds

4. Kim's scout troop earned 8
   points for every case of candy
   they sold. The troop sold 52
   cases. About how many points
   did they earn?

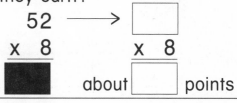

about _____ points

---

5. Mia threw a baseball 64 feet.
   Tom says he can throw a ball
   3 times as far as Mia threw.
   About how far does Tom think
   he can throw a baseball?

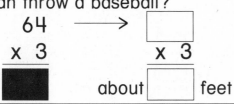

about _____ feet

6. Tyrone reads about 11 pages
   each day in his favorite book.
   About how many pages
   can he read in 4 days?

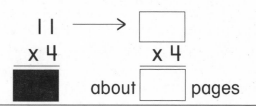

about _____ pages

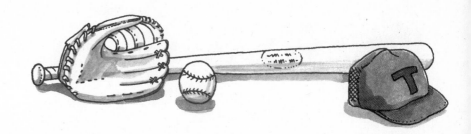

▷Multiply.

pages 76–77
1.   20
  × 3
	2. 400
	  × 2
		3. 50
		  × 3
			4. 10
			  × 9

pages 78–79
5.   33
  × 2
	6. 12
	  × 4
		7. 21
		  × 3
			8. 11
			  × 8

pages 80–81
9.   25
  × 3
	10. 15
	  × 4
		11. 45
		  × 2
			12. 16
			  × 5

13.   24
  × 3
	14. 38
	  × 2
		15. 27
		  × 2
			16. 17
			  × 4

pages 82–83
17.   26
  × 8
	18. 94
	  × 4
		19. 71
		  × 6
			20. 39
			  × 5

21.   63
  × 5
	22. 76
	  × 2
		23. 49
		  × 6
			24. 57
			  × 7

▶Multiply.

pages 84–85 25. $\begin{array}{r} 142 \\ \times\ \ 4 \\ \hline \end{array}$	26. $\begin{array}{r} 426 \\ \times\ \ 2 \\ \hline \end{array}$	27. $\begin{array}{r} 119 \\ \times\ \ 6 \\ \hline \end{array}$	28. $\begin{array}{r} 237 \\ \times\ \ 3 \\ \hline \end{array}$
29. $\begin{array}{r} 355 \\ \times\ \ 2 \\ \hline \end{array}$	30. $\begin{array}{r} 362 \\ \times\ \ 2 \\ \hline \end{array}$	31. $\begin{array}{r} 124 \\ \times\ \ 5 \\ \hline \end{array}$	32. $\begin{array}{r} 232 \\ \times\ \ 4 \\ \hline \end{array}$
pages 86–87 33. $\begin{array}{r} 461 \\ \times\ \ 8 \\ \hline \end{array}$	34. $\begin{array}{r} 522 \\ \times\ \ 6 \\ \hline \end{array}$	35. $\begin{array}{r} 430 \\ \times\ \ 5 \\ \hline \end{array}$	36. $\begin{array}{r} 319 \\ \times\ \ 7 \\ \hline \end{array}$
37. $\begin{array}{r} 352 \\ \times\ \ 3 \\ \hline \end{array}$	38. $\begin{array}{r} 246 \\ \times\ \ 5 \\ \hline \end{array}$	39. $\begin{array}{r} 768 \\ \times\ \ 4 \\ \hline \end{array}$	40. $\begin{array}{r} 635 \\ \times\ \ 7 \\ \hline \end{array}$

▶Ring A.M. or P.M.   pages 88–89

41. The sun is shining at 11:00.   A.M.   P.M.

42. Michael wakes up at 7:30.   A.M.   P.M.

43. The store opens at 10:00.   A.M.   P.M.

44. Leslie goes to bed at 9:30.   A.M.   P.M.

45. After school, the chorus meets at 4:00.   A.M.   P.M.

▶Round to the nearest ten.

Estimate to solve.

pages 90–91

---

46. There were 58 cookies in a package. Alice had 6 packages. About how many cookies in all did Alice have?

$$58 \longrightarrow \boxed{}$$
$$\underline{\times\ 6} \qquad \underline{\times\ 6}$$
■■■ about $\boxed{}$ cookies

47. A can of lemonade made 32 ounces. Robert bought 8 cans. About how many ounces of lemonade can Robert make?

$$32 \longrightarrow \boxed{}$$
$$\underline{\times\ 8} \qquad \underline{\times\ 8}$$
■■■ about $\boxed{}$ ounces

48. There were 89 straws in a box. Kiki had 3 boxes of straws. About how many straws in all were there?

$$89 \longrightarrow \boxed{}$$
$$\underline{\times\ 3} \qquad \underline{\times\ 3}$$
■■■ about $\boxed{}$ straws

49. There are 24 cups in a package. Lara has 7 packages. About how many cups in all are there?

$$24 \longrightarrow \boxed{}$$
$$\underline{\times\ 7} \qquad \underline{\times\ 7}$$
■■■ about $\boxed{}$ cups

50. There were 46 students at the picnic. Each student can have 2 hot dogs. About how many hot dogs in all are there?

$$46 \longrightarrow \boxed{}$$
$$\underline{\times\ 2} \qquad \underline{\times\ 2}$$
■■■ about $\boxed{}$ hot dogs

51. A watermelon can be cut into 62 slices. Sheku has 9 watermelons. About how many slices can Sheku cut?

$$62 \longrightarrow \boxed{}$$
$$\underline{\times\ 9} \qquad \underline{\times\ 9}$$
■■■ about $\boxed{}$ slices

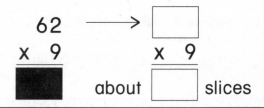

Multiply.

1. 30 × 3	2. 400 × 2	3. 11 × 3	4. 24 × 2
5. 26 × 3	6. 46 × 2	7. 32 × 8	8. 76 × 3
9. 276 × 3	10. 125 × 6	11. 418 × 2	12. 148 × 3
13. 283 × 4	14. 376 × 5	15. 508 × 7	16. 724 × 6

Ring A.M. or P.M.

17. Maria eats lunch at 12:15.   A.M.   P.M.

18. Martin gets dressed for school at 7:30.   A.M.   P.M.

19. After breakfast, Pat's father goes to work.   A.M.   P.M.

20. The last class at school ends at 2:30.   A.M.   P.M.

▷ Round to the nearest ten.
Estimate to solve.

---

21. Meg planted 24 seeds in a row.
She made 7 rows.
About how many plants in all
did Meg have?

$$24 \longrightarrow \boxed{}$$
$$\underline{\times\ 7} \qquad\quad \underline{\times\ 7}$$
$$\blacksquare \qquad \text{about } \boxed{} \text{ plants}$$

22. A shelf held 75 flower plants.
There are 3 shelves. How many
plants in all are there?

$$75 \longrightarrow \boxed{}$$
$$\underline{\times\ 3} \qquad\quad \underline{\times\ 3}$$
$$\blacksquare \qquad \text{about } \boxed{} \text{ plants}$$

23. A cucumber plant has
28 cucumbers. There are
2 plants. How many cucumbers
in all are there?

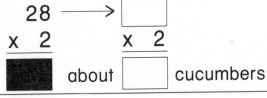

$$28 \longrightarrow \boxed{}$$
$$\underline{\times\ 2} \qquad\quad \underline{\times\ 2}$$
$$\blacksquare \qquad \text{about } \boxed{} \text{ cucumbers}$$

24. Kao has 36 packages of seedling
pots. Each package had
6 pots. About how many pots
in all did Kao have?

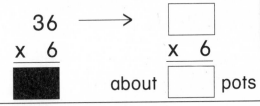

$$36 \longrightarrow \boxed{}$$
$$\underline{\times\ 6} \qquad\quad \underline{\times\ 6}$$
$$\blacksquare \qquad \text{about } \boxed{} \text{ pots}$$

25. Kim has 18 bags of potting soil.
Each bag weighs 5 pounds.
About how much in all do the
bags weigh?

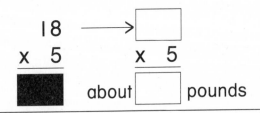

$$18 \longrightarrow \boxed{}$$
$$\underline{\times\ 5} \qquad\quad \underline{\times\ 5}$$
$$\blacksquare \qquad \text{about } \boxed{} \text{ pounds}$$

26. There are 57 feet of fencing
around the Garden Center.
Each section is 8 feet long.
About how many feet of fencing
in all are there?

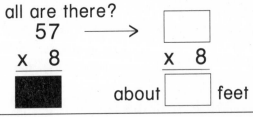

$$57 \longrightarrow \boxed{}$$
$$\underline{\times\ 8} \qquad\quad \underline{\times\ 8}$$
$$\blacksquare \qquad \text{about } \boxed{} \text{ feet}$$

5 Division Facts Through 9

▼   ▼   ▼   ▼   ▼   ▼   ▼

Andrew's baseball team scored 24 runs in 3 games. If they had the same score each time, how many runs did they score in each game?

Solve.

▷ Write a problem about a game you like to play.

_____

_____

_____

Dividing by 1, 2, 3, and 4

How many **threes** are in 12?

Step 1 Count: • • • • • • • • • • • •

Step 2 Divide:

12 divided by 3 equals 4.

$$4$$

Step 3 Write: $3\overline{)12}$ or $12 \div 3 = 4$

Step 4 Say: There are 4 **threes** in 12.

You can use a multiplication fact to find how many **threes** are in 12.
Since $4 \times 3 = 12$, you know that $12 \div 3 = 4$.

Any number ÷ 1 = that same number.
Any number ÷ itself = 1.

Guided Practice

▷Multiply. Then use the multiplication fact to help you divide.

1.	2.	3.	4.
$3 \times 3 = \underline{9}$	$5 \times 4 = \underline{}$	$7 \times 3 = \underline{}$	$6 \times 2 = \underline{}$
$3\overline{)9}$ $\,^3$	$4\overline{)20}$	$3\overline{)21}$	$2\overline{)12}$

Practice

▷ Divide.

1. $1\overline{)6}$	2. $3\overline{)18}$	3. $2\overline{)8}$	4. $4\overline{)16}$	5. $2\overline{)18}$
6. $3\overline{)27}$	7. $2\overline{)14}$	8. $1\overline{)9}$	9. $4\overline{)12}$	10. $3\overline{)6}$
11. $2\overline{)10}$	12. $3\overline{)24}$	13. $1\overline{)5}$	14. $4\overline{)8}$	15. $2\overline{)16}$

16. $3 \div 1 =$	17. $2 \div 2 =$	18. $12 \div 3 =$	19. $24 \div 4 =$

Using Math

▷ There are 24 students in Shawn's class. They are studying in groups of 3. How many groups of 3 are there?

There are _____ groups.

Work here.

Dividing by 5 and 6

How many **fives** are in 15? You can use a multiplication fact to answer this division question.

Multiplying fives				
1 × 5 = 5	2 × 5 = 10	**3 × 5 = 15**	4 × 5 = 15	5 × 5 = 25
6 × 5 = 30	7 × 5 = 35		8 × 5 = 40	9 × 5 = 45

Since 3 × 5 = 15, you know that 15 ÷ 5 = 3.
There are 3 **fives** in 15.

How many **sixes** are in 24?

Multiplying sixes				
1 × 6 = 6	2 × 6 = 12	3 × 6 = 18	**4 × 6 = 24**	5 × 6 = 30
6 × 6 = 36	7 × 6 = 42		8 × 6 = 48	9 × 6 = 54

Since 4 × 6 = 24, you know that 24 ÷ 6 = 4.
There are 4 **sixes** in 24.

Guided Practice

▶Multiply. Then use the multiplication fact to help you divide.

1.	2.	3.	4.
4 × 5 = <u>20</u>	1 × 6 = ___	7 × 6 = ___	3 × 6 = ___
$5\overline{)20}$ $\overset{4}{\phantom{5\overline{)20}}}$	$6\overline{)6}$	$6\overline{)42}$	18 ÷ 6 = ___

100

Practice

▷Divide.

1. $5\overline{)35}$	2. $6\overline{)42}$	3. $5\overline{)15}$	4. $6\overline{)48}$	5. $6\overline{)6}$
6. $5\overline{)45}$	7. $6\overline{)30}$	8. $5\overline{)25}$	9. $5\overline{)10}$	10. $4\overline{)16}$
11. $6\overline{)18}$	12. $5\overline{)5}$	13. $6\overline{)36}$	14. $6\overline{)24}$	15. $2\overline{)14}$

16. $40 \div 5 =$	17. $12 \div 6 =$	18. $30 \div 5 =$	19. $54 \div 6 =$

Using Math

▷Ana needs to buy 42 cups for the picnic. There are 6 cups in a package. How many packages should Ana buy?

Ana should buy _____ packages.

Work here.

101

Dividing by 7

How many **sevens** are in 21? You can use a multiplication fact to answer this division question.

Multiplying sevens				
$1 \times 7 = 7$	$2 \times 7 = 14$	$3 \times 7 = 21$	$4 \times 7 = 28$	$5 \times 7 = 35$
$6 \times 7 = 42$		$7 \times 7 = 49$	$8 \times 7 = 56$	$9 \times 7 = 63$

Since $3 \times 7 = 21$, you know that $21 \div 7 = 3$.
There are 3 **sevens** in 21.

Guided Practice

▷ Multiply. Then use the multiplication fact to help you divide.

1. $1 \times 7 = \underline{\quad 7 \quad}$ $7\overline{)7}^{\,1}$	2. $2 \times 7 = \underline{\quad\quad}$ $7\overline{)14}$	3. $3 \times 7 = \underline{\quad\quad}$ $7\overline{)21}$	4. $5 \times 7 = \underline{\quad\quad}$ $7\overline{)35}$
5. $7 \times 7 = \underline{\quad\quad}$ $49 \div 7 = \underline{\quad\quad}$	6. $4 \times 7 = \underline{\quad\quad}$ $28 \div 7 = \underline{\quad\quad}$	7. $9 \times 7 = \underline{\quad\quad}$ $63 \div 7 = \underline{\quad\quad}$	8. $6 \times 7 = \underline{\quad\quad}$ $42 \div 7 = \underline{\quad\quad}$

Practice

Divide.

1. 7)35	2. 7)42	3. 7)56	4. 2)14	5. 6)54
6. 7)63	7. 3)21	8. 4)20	9. 7)28	10. 4)12
11. 5)40	12. 5)35	13. 6)36	14. 7)49	15. 3)27

16.	17.	18.	19.
18 ÷ 2 =	42 ÷ 6 =	14 ÷ 7 =	24 ÷ 6 =

Using Math

The basketball team took a total of 56 practice shots. Each player took 7 shots. How many players are on the team?

There are _____ players on the team.

Work here.

Dividing by 8

How many **eights** are in 48? You can use a multiplication fact to answer this division question.

Multiplying eights				
$1 \times 8 = 8$	$2 \times 8 = 16$	$3 \times 8 = 24$	$4 \times 8 = 32$	$5 \times 8 = 40$
$6 \times 8 = 48$	$7 \times 8 = 56$		$8 \times 8 = 64$	$9 \times 8 = 72$

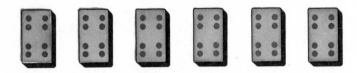

Since $6 \times 8 = 48$, you know that $48 \div 8 = 6$.
There are 6 **eights** in 48.

Guided Practice

▷ Multiply. Then use the multiplication fact to help you divide.

1. $4 \times 8 = \underline{\ 32\ }$ $\overset{4}{8)\overline{32}}$	2. $8 \times 8 = \underline{\quad}$ $8)\overline{64}$	3. $5 \times 8 = \underline{\quad}$ $8)\overline{40}$	4. $2 \times 8 = \underline{\quad}$ $8)\overline{16}$
5. $6 \times 8 = \underline{\quad}$ $48 \div 8 = \underline{\quad}$	6. $1 \times 8 = \underline{\quad}$ $8 \div 8 = \underline{\quad}$	7. $3 \times 8 = \underline{\quad}$ $24 \div 8 = \underline{\quad}$	8. $7 \times 8 = \underline{\quad}$ $56 \div 8 = \underline{\quad}$

Practice

▷ Divide.

1. $8\overline{)56}$	2. $8\overline{)16}$	3. $8\overline{)72}$	4. $7\overline{)56}$	5. $8\overline{)24}$
6. $5\overline{)40}$	7. $6\overline{)54}$	8. $3\overline{)24}$	9. $6\overline{)48}$	10. $7\overline{)42}$
11. $2\overline{)16}$	12. $4\overline{)16}$	13. $8\overline{)8}$	14. $4\overline{)32}$	15. $6\overline{)36}$

16. $40 \div 5 =$	17. $40 \div 8 =$	18. $32 \div 8 =$	19. $64 \div 8 =$

Problem Solving

▷ Round to the nearest ten.
Estimate to solve.

A movie theater has 38 rows of seats.
There are 8 seats in each row.
About how many seats in all are there?

$$38 \longrightarrow \boxed{}$$
$$\underline{\times\ 8} \qquad\quad \underline{\times\ 8}$$
$$\blacksquare \qquad \text{about } \boxed{} \text{ seats}$$

Dividing by 9

How many **nines** are in 36? You can use a multiplication fact to answer this division question.

Multiplying nines				
$1 \times 9 = 9$	$2 \times 9 = 18$	$3 \times 9 = 27$	$4 \times 9 = 36$	$5 \times 9 = 45$
$6 \times 9 = 54$	$7 \times 9 = 63$		$8 \times 9 = 72$	$9 \times 9 = 81$

Since $4 \times 9 = 36$, you know that $36 \div 9 = 4$.
There are 4 **nines** in 36.

Guided Practice

▷ Multiply. Then use the multiplication fact to help you divide.

1. $2 \times 9 = \underline{18}$ $9\overline{)18}$ (2)	2. $1 \times 9 = \underline{}$ $9\overline{)9}$	3. $4 \times 9 = \underline{}$ $9\overline{)36}$	4. $3 \times 9 = \underline{}$ $9\overline{)27}$
5. $9 \times 9 = \underline{}$ $81 \div 9 = \underline{}$	6. $7 \times 9 = \underline{}$ $63 \div 9 = \underline{}$	7. $8 \times 9 = \underline{}$ $72 \div 9 = \underline{}$	8. $6 \times 9 = \underline{}$ $54 \div 9 = \underline{}$

Practice

Divide.

1. $9\overline{)27}$	2. $9\overline{)54}$	3. $9\overline{)45}$	4. $6\overline{)54}$	5. $9\overline{)72}$
6. $4\overline{)32}$	7. $8\overline{)72}$	8. $9\overline{)81}$	9. $8\overline{)64}$	10. $7\overline{)28}$
11. $6\overline{)36}$	12. $5\overline{)20}$	13. $7\overline{)49}$	14. $3\overline{)27}$	15. $9\overline{)63}$

16. $56 \div 8 =$	17. $63 \div 7 =$	18. $72 \div 8 =$	19. $45 \div 5 =$

Using Math

There are 36 players on the baseball team. How many groups of 9 players can be made up for practice games?

_____ groups of 9 players can be made up for practice games.

Work here.

107

Multiplication and Division Facts

You know that multiplication facts can be used to find division facts.
Study the examples below.

Twos	$3 \times 2 = 6$ $6 \div 2 = 3$	$5 \times 2 = 10$ $10 \div 2 = 5$	$9 \times 2 = 18$ $18 \div 2 = 9$
Threes	$4 \times 3 = 12$ $12 \div 3 = 4$	$6 \times 3 = 18$ $18 \div 3 = 6$	$8 \times 3 = 24$ $24 \div 3 = 8$
Fours	$4 \times 4 = 16$ $16 \div 4 = 4$	$6 \times 4 = 24$ $24 \div 4 = 6$	$9 \times 4 = 36$ $36 \div 4 = 9$
Fives	$1 \times 5 = 5$ $5 \div 5 = 1$	$5 \times 5 = 25$ $25 \div 5 = 5$	$9 \times 5 = 45$ $45 \div 5 = 9$
Sixes	$4 \times 6 = 24$ $24 \div 6 = 4$	$6 \times 6 = 36$ $36 \div 6 = 6$	$8 \times 6 = 48$ $48 \div 6 = 8$
Sevens	$2 \times 7 = 14$ $14 \div 7 = 2$	$5 \times 7 = 35$ $35 \div 7 = 5$	$8 \times 7 = 56$ $56 \div 7 = 8$
Eights	$1 \times 8 = 8$ $8 \div 8 = 1$	$3 \times 8 = 24$ $24 \div 8 = 3$	$7 \times 8 = 56$ $56 \div 8 = 7$
Nines	$3 \times 9 = 27$ $27 \div 9 = 3$	$6 \times 9 = 54$ $54 \div 9 = 6$	$9 \times 9 = 81$ $81 \div 9 = 9$

Guided Practice

▷Multiply. Then divide.

1.	2.	3.	4.
$4 \times 2 = \underline{\ 8\ }$ $8 \div 2 = \underline{\ 4\ }$	$5 \times 3 = \underline{\quad}$ $15 \div 3 = \underline{\quad}$	$3 \times 4 = \underline{\quad}$ $12 \div 4 = \underline{\quad}$	$4 \times 6 = \underline{\quad}$ $24 \div 6 = \underline{\quad}$

Practice

▷ Multiply. Then divide.

1. $2 \times 2 =$ _____ $4 \div 2 =$ _____	2. $3 \times 3 =$ _____ $9 \div 3 =$ _____	3. $3 \times 4 =$ _____ $12 \div 4 =$ _____	4. $3 \times 5 =$ _____ $15 \div 5 =$ _____
5. $6 \times 5 =$ _____ $30 \div 5 =$ _____	6. $7 \times 6 =$ _____ $42 \div 6 =$ _____	7. $3 \times 8 =$ _____ $24 \div 8 =$ _____	8. $7 \times 3 =$ _____ $21 \div 3 =$ _____
9. $5 \times 9 =$ _____ $45 \div 9 =$ _____	10. $8 \times 2 =$ _____ $16 \div 2 =$ _____	11. $8 \times 4 =$ _____ $32 \div 4 =$ _____	12. $7 \times 4 =$ _____ $28 \div 4 =$ _____
13. $3 \times 6 =$ _____ $18 \div 6 =$ _____	14. $4 \times 7 =$ _____ $28 \div 7 =$ _____	15. $5 \times 7 =$ _____ $35 \div 7 =$ _____	16. $8 \times 9 =$ _____ $72 \div 9 =$ _____

Using Math

▷ Tim has 24 loose tennis balls.

Tim must put the balls away before he goes home.

3 balls will fit into a can.

How many cans will Tim need to put all the balls away?

Tim needs _____ cans to put all the balls away.

Work here.

109

Elapsed Time

Sometimes you need to know what time
it will be in a given number of minutes.

It is 7:15.

What time will it be in 10 minutes?

To find out, start
at the minute hand.
Count 10 more minutes.

It will be 7:25.

Guided Practice

▷ What time will it be?

1.	2.
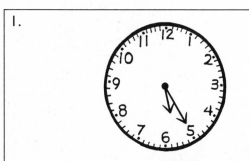	
In 10 minutes it will be _5:35_ .	In 5 minutes it will be _____ .

110

Practice

▷ Draw the minute hand to show time it will be. Then write the time.

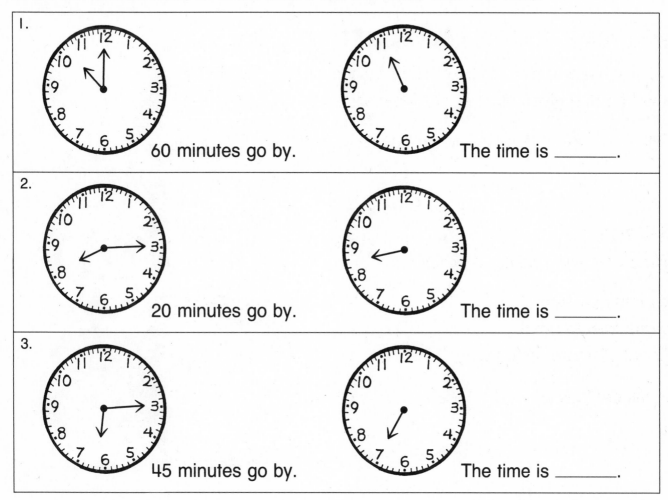

1.

60 minutes go by.

The time is _____.

2.

20 minutes go by.

The time is _____.

3.

45 minutes go by.

The time is _____.

Using Math

▷ It is 5:05 P.M. You tell your friends that you will meet them at Joe's Pizza Place in 35 minutes.

What time will you meet them? _____ P.M.
Draw the hands on the watch to show what time you will be at Joe's Pizza Place.

Problem Solving

Choose an Operation

Micki had 2 packages of hot dogs.
Each package had 8 hot dogs.
How many hot dogs did Micki have?

Micki multiplied because
she put the group of hot dogs together.

| Multiply to combine groups. |
| Divide to separate groups. |

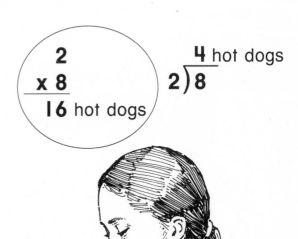

$$\begin{array}{r} 2 \\ \times\,8 \\ \hline 16 \text{ hot dogs} \end{array}$$

$$2\overline{)8}^{\,4\text{ hot dogs}}$$

Guided Practice

▷ Ring the correct problem.

---

1. James has 24 cookies.
   He gave an equal number of cookies
   to 4 friends. How many cookies
   did each friend get?

$$\begin{array}{r} 24 \\ \times\,4 \\ \hline 96 \text{ cookies} \end{array}$$

$$4\overline{)24}^{\,6\text{ cookies}}$$

James divided to separate the cookies into groups.

---

2. Takeo had 9 rows of plants.
   Each row had 3 plants.
   How many plants in all
   did Takeo have?

$$\begin{array}{r} 9 \\ \times\,3 \\ \hline 27 \text{ plants} \end{array}$$

$$3\overline{)9}^{\,3\text{ plants}}$$

112

Practice

▷ Ring the correct problem.

---

1. Amy had 9 books.
   She put them into 3 equal stacks.
   How many books
   were in each stack?

   $$\begin{array}{r} 9 \\ \times\ 3 \\ \hline 27 \end{array}\text{ books}$$

   $$3\overline{)9}\ \ ^{3}\text{ books}$$

---

2. Justin traded 18 baseball cards
   for some tapes.
   Each tape cost 9 baseball cards.
   How many tapes did Justin get?

   $$\begin{array}{r} 18 \\ \times\ 9 \\ \hline 162 \end{array}\text{ tapes}$$

   $$9\overline{)18}\ \ ^{2}\text{ tapes}$$

---

3. Seth had 5 packs of cards.
   Each pack had 10 cards.
   How many cards in all
   did Seth have?

   $$\begin{array}{r} 10 \\ \times\ 5 \\ \hline 50 \end{array}\text{ cards}$$

   $$5\overline{)10}\ \ ^{2}\text{ cards}$$

---

4. Akimi had 32 chairs.
   She put them in 4 equal rows.
   How many chairs
   did Akimi put in each row?

   $$\begin{array}{r} 32 \\ \times\ 4 \\ \hline 128 \end{array}\text{ chairs}$$

   $$4\overline{)32}\ \ ^{8}\text{ chairs}$$

---

5. Carrie had 2 sets of colored pencils.
   Each set had 8 pencils. How
   many colored pencils in all
   did Carrie have?

   $$\begin{array}{r} 8 \\ \times\ 2 \\ \hline 16 \end{array}\text{ pencils}$$

   $$2\overline{)8}\ \ ^{4}\text{ pencils}$$

CHAPTER 5 Review

▷Divide.

pages 98–99			
1. $2\overline{)14}$	2. $4\overline{)20}$	3. $1\overline{)9}$	4. $3\overline{)18}$
5. $1\overline{)6}$	6. $2\overline{)18}$	7. $3\overline{)21}$	8. $4\overline{)16}$
pages 100–101 9. $5\overline{)45}$	10. $6\overline{)12}$	11. $5\overline{)30}$	12. $6\overline{)24}$
13. $6\overline{)18}$	14. $5\overline{)25}$	15. $6\overline{)42}$	16. $5\overline{)10}$
pages 102–103 17. $7\overline{)7}$	18. $7\overline{)56}$	19. $7\overline{)14}$	20. $7\overline{)28}$
21. $7\overline{)35}$	22. $7\overline{)21}$	23. $7\overline{)49}$	24. $7\overline{)63}$

▷ Divide.

pages 104–105 25. 8)¯16¯	26. 8)¯40¯	27. 8)¯24¯	28. 8)¯32¯
29. 8)¯8¯	30. 8)¯48¯	31. 8)¯72¯	32. 8)¯56¯
pages 106–107 33. 9)¯27¯	34. 9)¯18¯	35. 9)¯45¯	36. 9)¯63¯
37. 9)¯36¯	38. 9)¯54¯	39. 9)¯81¯	40. 9)¯72¯

▷ What time will it be?   pages 110–111

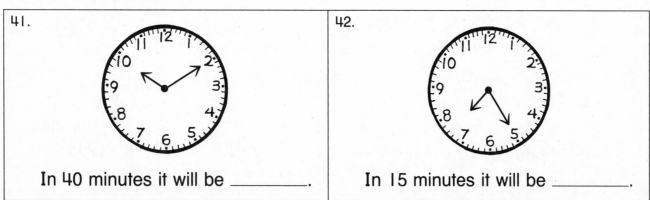

41. In 40 minutes it will be _____.

42. In 15 minutes it will be _____.

▷ Ring the correct problem.
pages 112–113

---

43. There were 24 students in Lino's class. They worked in groups of 6 students. How many groups were there in Lino's class?

$$\begin{array}{r} 24 \\ \times\ 6 \\ \hline 144 \end{array}$$ groups

$$6\overline{)24}$$ **4** groups

---

44. Sid's team got 2 touchdowns. They scored 6 points for each touchdown. How many points in all did they score?

$$\begin{array}{r} 6 \\ \times\ 2 \\ \hline 12 \end{array}$$ points

$$2\overline{)6}$$ **3** points

---

45. Ms. Mintz bought 6 packages of paintbrushes. Each package had 12 paintbrushes. How many paintbrushes in all did Ms. Mintz buy?

$$\begin{array}{r} 12 \\ \times\ 6 \\ \hline 72 \end{array}$$ paintbrushes

$$6\overline{)12}$$ **2** paintbrushes

---

46. Mr. Garza had 45 drawings. He put an equal number of drawings on 5 boards. How many drawings did Mr. Garza put on each board?

$$\begin{array}{r} 45 \\ \times\ 5 \\ \hline 225 \end{array}$$ drawings

$$5\overline{)45}$$ **9** drawings

---

47. Ernie baked 32 cookies. He gave an equal number of cookies to 8 friends. How many cookies did each friend get?

$$\begin{array}{r} 32 \\ \times\ 8 \\ \hline 256 \end{array}$$ cookies

$$8\overline{)32}$$ **4** cookies

▷Divide.

1. $2\overline{)10}$	2. $1\overline{)6}$	3. $3\overline{)15}$	4. $6\overline{)12}$
5. $7\overline{)21}$	6. $7\overline{)63}$	7. $7\overline{)28}$	8. $7\overline{)49}$
9. $8\overline{)64}$	10. $8\overline{)8}$	11. $8\overline{)48}$	12. $8\overline{)40}$
13. $9\overline{)27}$	14. $9\overline{)63}$	15. $9\overline{)81}$	16. $9\overline{)36}$

▷What time will it be?

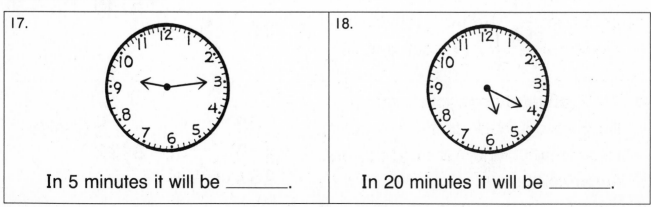

17.	18.
In 5 minutes it will be _____.	In 20 minutes it will be _____.

▶Ring the correct problem.

---

19. Jordan had 4 boxes of microwave popcorn. Each box had 8 bags of popcorn. How many bags of popcorn in all did Jordan have?

    8
  x 4
  32 bags

    2 bags
4)8

---

20. Jackie had 12 slices of pizza. She shared the pizza equally among 4 people. How many slices of pizza did each person get?

  12
 x 4
 48 slices

    3 slices
4)12

---

21. The animal shelter had 3 litters of kittens. Each litter had 6 kittens. How many kittens in all were there?

   6
 x 3
 18 kittens

   2 kittens
3)6

---

22. Mr. Gale put 35 new bikes in racks. Each rack held 5 bikes. How many racks did Mr. Gale fill?

  35
 x 5
 175 racks

   7 racks
5)35

---

23. Pele bought 3 cases of juice. Each case had 12 cans of juice. How many cans of juice did Pele buy?

  12
 x 3
 36 cans

   4 cans
3)12

---

6 Dividing with 1-Digit Divisors

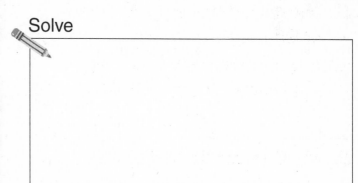

Chad, Mario, and Amy shared a pizza that was cut into 8 pieces. Each of them ate the same number of pieces. How many pieces of pizza did each one of them eat? How many were left over?

Solve

▷ Write a problem about something you like to share.

_____

_____

_____

_____

Division with Remainders

Sometimes you have an amount left over when you divide.

Step 1	Step 2	Step 3
Divide 9 by 2. $2\overline{)9}$ How many groups of 2 are in 9? There are 4 groups of 2 in 9. $\begin{array}{r} 4 \\ 2\overline{)9} \end{array}$	**Multiply** 4 by 2. $4 \times 2 = 8$ Place the 8 under the 9. $\begin{array}{r} 4 \\ 2\overline{)9} \\ \underline{8} \end{array}$	**Subtract** 8 from 9. $9 - 8 = 1$ $\begin{array}{r} 4 \\ 2\overline{)9} \\ -\,8 \\ \hline 1 \end{array}$

The amount left over is the **remainder.**
It is written with the **quotient.**

$\begin{array}{r} 4 \text{ R1} \leftarrow \text{remainder} \\ 2\overline{)9} \\ -\,8 \\ \hline 1 \end{array}$

Guided Practice

▷Divide.

1. $\begin{array}{r} 3 \text{ R1} \\ 5\overline{)16} \\ -15 \\ \hline 1 \end{array}$	2. $2\overline{)11}$	3. $3\overline{)13}$	4. $2\overline{)19}$	5. $2\overline{)9}$

120

Practice

Divide.

1. $4\overline{)13}$	2. $6\overline{)37}$	3. $2\overline{)11}$	4. $7\overline{)50}$	5. $9\overline{)46}$
6. $3\overline{)19}$	7. $8\overline{)25}$	8. $5\overline{)36}$	9. $9\overline{)64}$	10. $6\overline{)49}$
11. $6\overline{)13}$	12. $2\overline{)7}$	13. $4\overline{)29}$	14. $7\overline{)43}$	15. $2\overline{)19}$

Using Math

Ellen bought 3 pencils and paid for them with a quarter. She got 1¢ in change. How much did each pencil cost?

Each pencil cost _____ ¢.

121

Dividing Tens and Hundreds

You know that 8 ones ÷ 2 ones = 4 ones.

$$2\overline{)8}^{\,4}$$

Now you can find the answer to division problems with tens and hundreds.

tens	hundreds

Divide 80 by 2.
   Think 80 = 8 tens.
 	
     $2\overline{)8\text{ tens}}^{\,4\text{ tens}}$ or $2\overline{)80}^{\,40}$
	Divide 800 by 2.
	   Think 800 = 8 hundreds.
	
	     $2\overline{)8\text{ hundreds}}^{\,4\text{ hundreds}}$ or $2\overline{)800}^{\,400}$

Divide 60 by 3.
   Think 60 = 6 tens.
 	
     $3\overline{)6\text{ tens}}^{\,2\text{ tens}}$ or $3\overline{)60}^{\,20}$
	Divide 600 by 3.
	   Think 600 = 6 hundreds.
	
	     $3\overline{)6\text{ hundreds}}^{\,2\text{ hundreds}}$ or $3\overline{)600}^{\,200}$

Guided Practice

▷Divide.

1. $2\overline{)6\text{ tens}}^{\,3\text{ tens}}$	2. $3\overline{)9\text{ tens}}$	3. $2\overline{)8\text{ hundreds}}$	4. $3\overline{)6\text{ hundreds}}$
5. $7\overline{)700}$	6. $2\overline{)60}$	7. $5\overline{)50}$	8. $4\overline{)200}$

Practice

▷ Divide.

1. $2\overline{)40}$	2. $2\overline{)400}$	3. $5\overline{)500}$	4. $3\overline{)90}$	5. $2\overline{)80}$
6. $6\overline{)600}$	7. $4\overline{)40}$	8. $8\overline{)80}$	9. $3\overline{)30}$	10. $4\overline{)80}$
11. $3\overline{)300}$	12. $4\overline{)400}$	13. $2\overline{)60}$	14. $2\overline{)600}$	15. $2\overline{)800}$
16. $5\overline{)400}$	17. $7\overline{)70}$	18. $6\overline{)300}$	19. $4\overline{)800}$	20. $3\overline{)900}$

Using Math

▷ Craig bought a book with 90 pages in it. The book had 9 equal chapters. How many pages are in each chapter?

There are _____ pages in each chapter.

2-Digit Quotients

You know how to divide 60 by 2. Now you will learn to divide 68 by 2.

Step 1 ▷ Divide the tens.	**Step 2** ▷ Divide the ones.
Divide 6 by 2.	▶ **Bring down the 8 ones.**
$6 \div 2 = 3$	

$$\begin{array}{r} 3 \\ 2{\overline{)68}} \\ -6 \\ \hline 0 \end{array}$$

Multiply 3 times 2.

$3 \times 2 = 6$

Subtract 6 from 6.

$6 - 6 = 0$

Step 2 ▷ Divide the ones.

▶ **Bring down the 8 ones.**

Divide 8 by 2.

$8 \div 2 = 4$

$$\begin{array}{r} 34 \\ 2{\overline{)68}} \\ -6\downarrow \\ \hline 08 \\ -8 \\ \hline 0 \end{array}$$

Multiply 4 times 2.

$4 \times 2 = 8$

Subtract 8 from 8.

$8 - 8 = 0$

Guided Practice

▷ Divide.

1.	2.	3.	4.	5.
$\begin{array}{r} 12 \\ 2{\overline{)24}} \\ -2 \\ \hline 04 \\ -4 \\ \hline 0 \end{array}$	$3{\overline{)66}}$	$4{\overline{)48}}$	$5{\overline{)55}}$	$6{\overline{)60}}$

Practice

▷ Divide.

1. $2\overline{)26}$	2. $3\overline{)93}$	3. $5\overline{)50}$	4. $4\overline{)44}$	5. $2\overline{)48}$
6. $4\overline{)84}$	7. $8\overline{)88}$	8. $2\overline{)22}$	9. $2\overline{)64}$	10. $3\overline{)39}$
11. $7\overline{)70}$	12. $4\overline{)88}$	13. $3\overline{)36}$	14. $9\overline{)90}$	15. $3\overline{)63}$

Using Math

▷ Yoshi runs 2 miles every day. How many days will it take her to run 24 miles?

It will take her _____ days.

2-Digit Quotients with Remainders

When 36 is divided by 3, there is no remainder.

$$\begin{array}{r} 12 \\ 3\overline{)36} \end{array}$$

When 37 is divided by 3, there is a remainder of 1.

Step 1 Divide the tens.	**Step 2** Divide the ones.
Divide $\quad 3 \div 3 \qquad 1$	Bring down the 7 ones. $\qquad$ 12
$\qquad\qquad\qquad 3\overline{)37}$	**Divide** $\quad 7 \div 3 \qquad 3\overline{)37}$
Multiply $\quad 1 \times 3 \qquad -3$	$\qquad\qquad\qquad\qquad -3\downarrow$
Subtract $\quad 3 - 3 \qquad \overline{\;0\;}$	**Multiply** $\quad 2 \times 3 \qquad \overline{07}$
	Subtract $\quad 7 - 6 \qquad -6$
	$\qquad\qquad\qquad\qquad \overline{\;1\;}$

Remember to write the remainder like this:
$$\begin{array}{r} 12\ \text{R1} \\ 3\overline{)37} \end{array}$$

Guided Practice

▷Divide.

1. $\begin{array}{r} 12\ R1 \\ 2\overline{)25} \\ -2 \\ \overline{05} \\ -4 \\ \overline{\;1\;} \end{array}$	2. $3\overline{)34}$	3. $4\overline{)87}$	4. $3\overline{)64}$	5. $4\overline{)46}$

126

Practice

▷Divide.

1. $3\overline{)64}$	2. $4\overline{)87}$	3. $2\overline{)85}$	4. $5\overline{)56}$	5. $3\overline{)67}$
6. $2\overline{)29}$	7. $6\overline{)68}$	8. $2\overline{)65}$	9. $4\overline{)89}$	10. $2\overline{)23}$
11. $7\overline{)78}$	12. $2\overline{)87}$	13. $8\overline{)89}$	14. $4\overline{)85}$	15. $4\overline{)49}$

Using Math

▷There are 85 people waiting at the bus station. A bus can hold 42 people. Can 2 buses carry all the people?

Ring your answer.   Yes   No

2-Digit Quotients with Remainders

Divide 91 by 4. $4\overline{)91}$

Step 1 Divide the tens.	Step 2 Divide the ones.
Divide $9 \div 4$ 2	Bring down the 1. 22
Multiply 2×4 $4\overline{)91}$	**Divide** $11 \div 4$ $4\overline{)91}$
Subtract $9 - 8$ $\begin{array}{r}-8 \\ \hline 1\end{array}$	**Multiply** 2×4 $\begin{array}{r}-8\downarrow \\ \hline 11\end{array}$
Is 1 less than 4? Yes.	**Subtract** $11 - 8$ $\begin{array}{r}-8 \\ \hline 3\end{array}$
Go on to Step 2.	

Remember to write the remainder like this: $4\overline{)91}^{\,22\text{ R}3}$

Guided Practice

▷Divide.

1.	2.	3.	4.	5.
$\begin{array}{r}14\text{ R}3 \\ 4\overline{)59} \\ -4 \\ \hline 19 \\ -16 \\ \hline 3\end{array}$	$5\overline{)83}$	$3\overline{)86}$	$6\overline{)95}$	$2\overline{)75}$

Practice

▶Divide.

1. $3\overline{)43}$	2. $4\overline{)51}$	3. $5\overline{)86}$	4. $6\overline{)89}$	5. $7\overline{)99}$
6. $3\overline{)76}$	7. $4\overline{)97}$	8. $8\overline{)99}$	9. $2\overline{)91}$	10. $3\overline{)89}$
11. $3\overline{)82}$	12. $5\overline{)89}$	13. $3\overline{)68}$	14. $4\overline{)63}$	15. $6\overline{)98}$

Using Math

▶Mr. Simms is baking 74 granola squares for his class. Each

student will get 4. How many students are in the class? _____

How many granola squares will be left for Mr. Simms? _____

2-Digit Quotients with Remainders

Divide 195 by 4. $4\overline{)195}$

Can you divide 1 by 4? No.

Think   195 = 1 hundred 9 tens 5 ones or 19 tens 5 ones.

Can you divide 19 tens by 4? Yes.

Step 1 Divide the tens.	**Step 2** Divide the ones.
Divide 19 tens by 4. 4 Remember to place the 4 $4\overline{)195}$ over the 9. This is the -16 tens' place. 3 **Multiply** 4×4 **Subtract** $19 - 16$ Is 3 less than 4? Yes. Go on to Step 2.	Bring down the 5. 48 R3 **Divide** $35 \div 4$ $4\overline{)195}$ **Multiply** 8×4 $-16\downarrow$ **Subtract** $35 - 32$ 35 Write R3 with the -32 quotient. 3

Guided Practice

▷Divide.

1. 66 R2 $4\overline{)266}$ -24 26 -24 2	2. $3\overline{)235}$	3. $7\overline{)376}$	4. $6\overline{)411}$

Practice

▶Divide.

1. $6\overline{)169}$	2. $5\overline{)243}$	3. $3\overline{)172}$	4. $7\overline{)388}$
5. $8\overline{)475}$	6. $8\overline{)578}$	7. $4\overline{)391}$	8. $3\overline{)268}$
9. $5\overline{)422}$	10. $7\overline{)265}$	11. $8\overline{)734}$	12. $9\overline{)829}$

Problem Solving

▶Ring the correct problem.

Chet had 3 packages of gum.
Each package had 6 pieces of gum.
How many pieces of gum in all
did Chet have?

$$\begin{array}{r} 6 \\ \times\ 3 \\ \hline 18 \text{ pieces} \end{array}$$

$$\begin{array}{r} 2 \text{ pieces} \\ 3\overline{)6} \end{array}$$

More Elapsed Time

Carlos is baking muffins. He puts them in the oven at 6:28 P.M. The muffins must bake for 20 minutes. What time will they be done?

Start Time
6:28

End Time
6:48

20 minutes

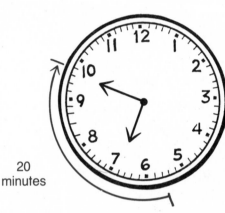

The muffins will be done at 6:48 P.M.

Guided Practice

▷ Write each answer.

1. The race began at 2:00 P.M.
   The winner finished the race at 2:32 P.M.
   How many minutes did the winner run?

   <u> 32 </u> minutes

   Start Time

2. It takes Betty 17 minutes to ride
   to Carol's house on her bicycle.
   She left at 10:05 P.M.

   What time will she get there? _____ P.M.

   Start Time

Practice

▷ Write each answer.

---

1. The bus stopped at Grove Street at 8:12 P.M.
   It arrived at Mason Road at 8:34 P.M.
   How many minutes did it take the bus to
   get from Grove Street to Mason Road?

   _____ minutes

   Start Time
   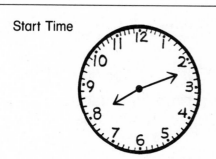

---

2. Band practice starts at 3:00 P.M.
   It will last 55 minutes. What time
   will practice end?

   _____ P.M.

   Start Time
   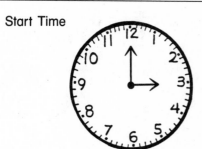

---

3. It is now 3:42 P.M. Mike's favorite TV show
   begins at 4:00 P.M. How many minutes will
   go by before Mike's show begins?

   _____ minutes

   Start Time
   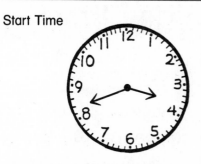

Using Math

▷ What time do you leave for school? _____

How many minutes does it take to get there? _____

What time do you get to school? _____

Problem Solving

Choose an Operation

Erin had 200 pennies.
She put them into 4 rolls.
How many pennies were in each roll?

$$\begin{array}{r} 200 \\ \times\ 4 \\ \hline 800 \end{array} \text{ pennies}$$

Erin divided because
she separated the pennies into groups.

> Multiply to combine groups.
> Divide to separate groups.

Guided Practice

▷ Ring the correct problem.

---

1. Amelia sold 24 boxes of cards.
   Each box had 6 cards.
   How many cards in all
   did Amelia sell?

   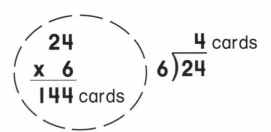

   Amelia multiplied because
   she put the groups of cards together.

---

2. Hal's book has 120 pages.
   Hal reads 8 pages each day.
   How many days will it take
   for Hal to read his book?

   $$\begin{array}{r} 120 \\ \times\ 8 \\ \hline 960 \end{array} \text{ days}$$

   $$8\overline{)120}\ \ ^{15}\text{ days}$$

Practice

▷Ring the correct problem.

---

1. Mr. Polk packed 6 lunches.
   He put 3 cookies in each lunch.
   How many cookies in all
   did Mr. Polk pack?

   $$\begin{array}{r} 6 \\ \times\ 3 \\ \hline 18 \end{array}$$ cookies

   $$3\overline{)6}$$ 2 cookies

---

2. Kelly works in a grocery store.
   She unpacked 6 cases of soup.
   Each case had 24 cans. How many
   cans in all did Kelly unpack?

   $$\begin{array}{r} 24 \\ \times\ 6 \\ \hline 144 \end{array}$$ cans

   $$6\overline{)24}$$ 4 cans

---

3. Tim packed 100 grapes for a picnic.
   He put 10 grapes in each package.
   How many packages
   did Tim make?

   $$\begin{array}{r} 100 \\ \times\ 10 \\ \hline 1,000 \end{array}$$ packages

   $$10\overline{)100}$$ 10 packages

---

4. Taizo brought 36 colas to a picnic.
   The colas were in 6 pack cartons.
   How many cartons of colas
   did Taizo bring?

   $$\begin{array}{r} 36 \\ \times\ 6 \\ \hline 216 \end{array}$$ cartons

   $$6\overline{)36}$$ 6 cartons

---

5. Ms. Andrews' class played softball.
   They made 2 equal teams.
   There were 22 students playing.
   How many students were on
   each team?

   $$\begin{array}{r} 22 \\ \times\ 2 \\ \hline 44 \end{array}$$ students

   $$2\overline{)22}$$ 11 students

▷Divide.

pages 120–121			
1. $2\overline{)17}$	2. $3\overline{)10}$	3. $5\overline{)26}$	4. $7\overline{)15}$
pages 122–123			
5. $2\overline{)40}$	6. $3\overline{)600}$	7. $4\overline{)400}$	8. $4\overline{)80}$
pages 124–125			
9. $2\overline{)42}$	10. $3\overline{)36}$	11. $4\overline{)44}$	12. $2\overline{)28}$
pages 126–127			
13. $3\overline{)34}$	14. $4\overline{)45}$	15. $2\overline{)29}$	16. $3\overline{)67}$

▷ Divide.

pages 128–129			
17. $3\overline{)43}$	18. $8\overline{)92}$	19. $4\overline{)54}$	20. $6\overline{)75}$
pages 130–131 21. $4\overline{)191}$	22. $3\overline{)235}$	23. $8\overline{)269}$	24. $6\overline{)519}$

▷ Write each answer.   pages 132–133

25. It is now 3:10. Louis is meeting his friends at the park at 3:30. How many minutes does Louis have left before he meets his friends?

He has _____ minutes left.

Start Time
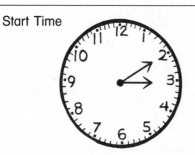

26. It is now 6:15 P.M. Tammy's father said dinner will be ready in 25 minutes. What time will dinner be ready?

Dinner will be ready at _____ P.M.

Start Time
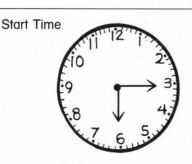

▷Ring the correct problem.

pages 134–135

---

27. Ryan bought 2 pens.
Each pen cost 18¢.
How much in all
did Ryan spend?

$$\begin{array}{r} 18¢ \\ \times\ 2 \\ \hline 36¢ \end{array}$$

$$\begin{array}{r} 9¢ \\ 2\overline{)18¢} \end{array}$$

---

28. Jordi had a book with 112 pages.
He read 8 pages each day.
How many days did it take him
to read the whole book?

$$\begin{array}{r} 112 \\ \times\ 8 \\ \hline 896 \end{array}\ \text{days}$$

$$\begin{array}{r} 14\,\text{days} \\ 8\overline{)112} \end{array}$$

---

29. Stef drove 55 miles each hour.
How many miles did she drive
in 3 hours?

$$\begin{array}{r} 55 \\ \times\ 3 \\ \hline 165 \end{array}\ \text{miles}$$

$$\begin{array}{r} 18\ \text{R}\ 1\ \text{miles} \\ 3\overline{)55} \end{array}$$

---

30. Ying's school had 424 students.
There were 8 students in each
activity group.
How many groups were there?

$$\begin{array}{r} 424 \\ \times\ 8 \\ \hline 3,392 \end{array}\ \text{groups}$$

$$\begin{array}{r} 53\,\text{groups} \\ 8\overline{)424} \end{array}$$

---

31. Ms. Sandoz set up 7 rows of chairs
for the school play. She put
14 chairs in each row. How
many chairs did Ms. Sandoz set up?

$$\begin{array}{r} 14 \\ \times\ 7 \\ \hline 98 \end{array}\ \text{chairs}$$

$$\begin{array}{r} 2\ \text{chairs} \\ 7\overline{)14} \end{array}$$

▷Divide.

1. $3\overline{)19}$	2. $5\overline{)31}$	3. $8\overline{)80}$	4. $6\overline{)600}$
5. $3\overline{)39}$	6. $2\overline{)24}$	7. $4\overline{)49}$	8. $3\overline{)67}$
9. $6\overline{)74}$	10. $3\overline{)49}$	11. $6\overline{)256}$	12. $5\overline{)369}$

▷Write the answer.

13. It is now 7:30 P.M. The movie will end
in 15 minutes. What time will the movie end?

The movie will end at _____ P.M.

Start Time

139

▷ Ring the correct problem.

---

14. Jerry gave a bag of spice drops to 6 friends. There were 72 spice drops in the bag. How many spice drops did each friend get?

$$\begin{array}{r} 72 \\ \times\ 6 \\ \hline 432 \end{array}$$ spice drops

$$6\overline{)72}$$ 12 spice drops

---

15. An address book had 156 pages. There were spaces for 4 addresses on each page. How many spaces in all were there?

$$\begin{array}{r} 156 \\ \times\ 4 \\ \hline 624 \end{array}$$ spaces

$$4\overline{)156}$$ 39 spaces

---

16. Jasmine drove 42 miles each hour. How many miles did she drive in 6 hours?

$$\begin{array}{r} 42 \\ \times\ 6 \\ \hline 252 \end{array}$$ miles

$$6\overline{)42}$$ 7 miles

---

17. Music City Store had 152 new tapes. They put an equal number on 8 shelves. How many new tapes are on each shelf?

$$\begin{array}{r} 152 \\ \times\ 8 \\ \hline 1{,}216 \end{array}$$ new tapes

$$8\overline{)152}$$ 19 new tapes

---

18. Chelsea had 16 flower seeds. She planted the same number of seeds in 4 flower pots. How many seeds did she plant in each pot?

$$\begin{array}{r} 16 \\ \times\ 4 \\ \hline 64 \end{array}$$ seeds

$$4\overline{)16}$$ 4 seeds

140

▷Multiply.

pages 76–79			
1. $\begin{array}{r} 10 \\ \times\ 8 \\ \hline \end{array}$	2. $\begin{array}{r} 200 \\ \times\ 4 \\ \hline \end{array}$	3. $\begin{array}{r} 21 \\ \times\ 3 \\ \hline \end{array}$	4. $\begin{array}{r} 42 \\ \times\ 2 \\ \hline \end{array}$
pages 80–83			
5. $\begin{array}{r} 16 \\ \times\ 3 \\ \hline \end{array}$	6. $\begin{array}{r} 27 \\ \times\ 2 \\ \hline \end{array}$	7. $\begin{array}{r} 68 \\ \times\ 3 \\ \hline \end{array}$	8. $\begin{array}{r} 95 \\ \times\ 5 \\ \hline \end{array}$
pages 84–85			
9. $\begin{array}{r} 243 \\ \times\ 4 \\ \hline \end{array}$	10. $\begin{array}{r} 152 \\ \times\ 6 \\ \hline \end{array}$	11. $\begin{array}{r} 371 \\ \times\ 2 \\ \hline \end{array}$	12. $\begin{array}{r} 273 \\ \times\ 3 \\ \hline \end{array}$
pages 86–87			
13. $\begin{array}{r} 263 \\ \times\ 7 \\ \hline \end{array}$	14. $\begin{array}{r} 152 \\ \times\ 9 \\ \hline \end{array}$	15. $\begin{array}{r} 403 \\ \times\ 5 \\ \hline \end{array}$	16. $\begin{array}{r} 619 \\ \times\ 4 \\ \hline \end{array}$

▷Ring A.M. or P.M.   pages 88–89

17. Pedro eats breakfast at 7:30.   A.M.   P.M.

18. Julia goes to ballet class at 4:00.   A.M.   P.M.

19. School gets out at 3:30.   A.M.   P.M.

20. Michael does his homework at 5:00.   A.M.   P.M.

▷Round to the nearest ten.
Estimate to solve.
pages 90–91

---

21. The park had 42 visitors.
Each visitor got 2 free
movie passes. About how
many passes were given away?

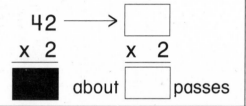

42 ⟶ ☐
x 2   x 2
■   about ☐ passes

22. There are 8 flights of steps
going up to the falls. Each flight
has 26 steps. About how many
steps in all are there?

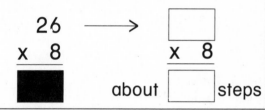

26 ⟶ ☐
x 8   x 8
■   about ☐ steps

---

23. A movie was shown 6 times a
day. The movie is 17 minutes
long. About how many minutes
was the movie projector
running in a day?

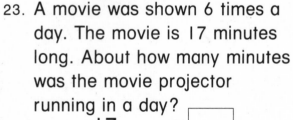

17 ⟶ ☐
x 6   x 6
■   about ☐ minutes

24. The snack bar is open 85
days a year. Each day it is
open 3 hours. About how
many hours is the snack bar
open in a year?

85 ⟶ ☐
x 3   x 3
■   about ☐ hours

---

25. On Tuesday 7 bus loads of
people visited the park. Each
bus held 47 people. About how
many people rode the bus to the
park on Tuesday?

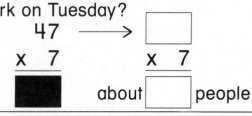

47 ⟶ ☐
x 7   x 7
■   about ☐ people

26. There were 4 tour guides.
Each guide led a group of 39
people. About how many
people were with the tour
guides?

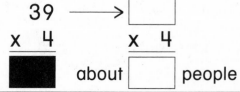

39 ⟶ ☐
x 4   x 4
■   about ☐ people

▷ Divide.

pages 98–101 1. $5\overline{)25}$	2. $3\overline{)27}$	3. $6\overline{)24}$	4. $4\overline{)16}$
pages 102–103 5. $7\overline{)21}$	6. $7\overline{)42}$	7. $7\overline{)14}$	8. $7\overline{)63}$
pages 104–105 9. $8\overline{)56}$	10. $8\overline{)40}$	11. $8\overline{)24}$	12. $8\overline{)72}$
pages 106–109 13. $9\overline{)27}$	14. $9\overline{)45}$	15. $9\overline{)18}$	16. $9\overline{)81}$

▷ What time will it be?   pages 110–111

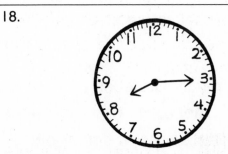

17.

In 5 minutes it will be _____.

18.

In 30 minutes it will be _____.

143

▶Ring the correct problem.
pages 112–113

---

19. A van held 15 people. It had 5 seats. How many people can sit in each seat?

$$\begin{array}{r} 15 \\ \times\ 5 \\ \hline 75 \end{array}\text{ people}$$

$$5\overline{)15}\ \ \overset{3}{}\text{ people}$$

---

20. Mei bought 2 packs of gum. Each pack had 6 pieces of gum. How many pieces of gum in all did Mei have?

$$\begin{array}{r} 6 \\ \times\ 2 \\ \hline 12 \end{array}\text{ pieces}$$

$$2\overline{)6}\ \ \overset{3}{}\text{ pieces}$$

---

21. Luis had 30 minutes to finish his math problems. He had 6 problems. How many minutes did Luis spend on each problem?

$$\begin{array}{r} 30 \\ \times\ 6 \\ \hline 180 \end{array}\text{ minutes}$$

$$6\overline{)30}\ \ \overset{5}{}\text{ minutes}$$

---

22. Ali made 2 pancakes for each person in her family. There are 6 people in Ali's family. How many pancakes did she make?

$$\begin{array}{r} 2 \\ \times\ 6 \\ \hline 12 \end{array}\text{ pancakes}$$

$$2\overline{)6}\ \ \overset{3}{}\text{ pancakes}$$

---

23. Sacho bought 3 pieces of candy for each friend. He had 12 friends. How many pieces of candy did Sacho buy?

$$\begin{array}{r} 12 \\ \times\ 3 \\ \hline 36 \end{array}\text{ pieces}$$

$$3\overline{)12}\ \ \overset{4}{}\text{ pieces}$$

▷ Divide.

pages 120–123 1. $4\overline{)25}$	2. $3\overline{)13}$	3. $3\overline{)60}$	4. $7\overline{)700}$
pages 124–127 5. $4\overline{)44}$	6. $3\overline{)36}$	7. $2\overline{)83}$	8. $4\overline{)49}$
pages 128–131 9. $5\overline{)66}$	10. $4\overline{)87}$	11. $8\overline{)387}$	12. $3\overline{)245}$

▷ Write the answer.   pages 132–133

13. Mr. Clark takes the train to work. He gets on
the train at 8:10 P.M. The train ride takes 40 minutes.
What time does he get off the train?

He gets off the train at _____ P.M.

Start Time

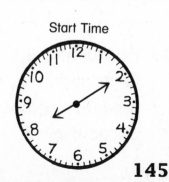

145

▶Ring the correct problem.

pages 134–135

---

14. A bag of cookies had 98 cookies. Ms. Brown bought 2 bags of cookies. How many cookies in all did Ms. Brown buy?

$$\begin{array}{r} 98 \\ \times\ 2 \\ \hline 196 \end{array}\text{ cookies}$$

$$\begin{array}{r} 49 \\ 2\overline{)98} \end{array}\text{ cookies}$$

---

15. Matt had 84 cards. He put them in 6 equal rows. How many rows of cards did Matt have?

$$\begin{array}{r} 84 \\ \times\ 6 \\ \hline 504 \end{array}\text{ rows}$$

$$\begin{array}{r} 14 \\ 6\overline{)84} \end{array}\text{ rows}$$

---

16. Paul had 268 tomatoes. He put them in packages of 4 tomatoes. How many packages of tomatoes did Paul have?

$$\begin{array}{r} 268 \\ \times\ 4 \\ \hline 1{,}072 \end{array}\text{ packages}$$

$$\begin{array}{r} 67 \\ 4\overline{)268} \end{array}\text{ packages}$$

---

17. A factory made wheels for roller skates. Each skate had 4 wheels. How many wheels did they need for 300 skates?

$$\begin{array}{r} 300 \\ \times\ 4 \\ \hline 1{,}200 \end{array}\text{ wheels}$$

$$\begin{array}{r} 75 \\ 4\overline{)300} \end{array}\text{ wheels}$$

---

18. Jan had 6 boxes of greeting cards. There were 12 cards in each box. How many cards in all did Jan have?

$$\begin{array}{r} 12 \\ \times\ 6 \\ \hline 72 \end{array}\text{ cards}$$

$$\begin{array}{r} 2 \\ 6\overline{)12} \end{array}\text{ cards}$$

146

▷ Write each missing number. pages 2–3

1. 64 = _____ tens _____ ones

2. 75 = _____ tens _____ ones

▷ Write each number in standard form. pages 4–5

3. 6,000 + 700 + 50 + 9 = _____

4. 1,000 + 300 + 80 = _____

▷ Write the value of each underlined digit. pages 6–7

5. 8<u>3</u>,622 _____

6. <u>3</u>6,521 _____

▷ Compare. Ring > or <. pages 8–9

7. 175 $\overset{>}{\underset{<}{}}$ 157

8. 3,825 $\overset{>}{\underset{<}{}}$ 8,352

9. 63,541 $\overset{>}{\underset{<}{}}$ 63,632

▷ Round each number to the nearest ten. pages 10–13

10. 11 _____

11. 26 _____

12. 185 _____

▷ Round each number to the nearest hundred. pages 12–13

13. 819 _____

14. 290 _____

15. 4,679 _____

▷ Round each number to the nearest thousand. pages 12–13

16. 2,436 _____

17. 6,555 _____

18. 36,213 _____

▷ Write each time. pages 14–15

19.	20.	21.

_____	_____	_____

Mr. Lock's class asked students to name their favorite hobbies. They used their answers to make this graph.

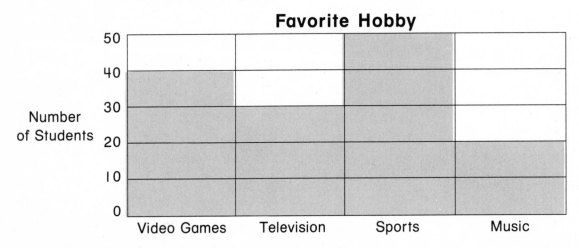

Favorite Hobby

Number of Students

Video Games   Television   Sports   Music

▷ Look at the graph.

Write how many students named the hobby.

pages 16–17

| 22. _____ Television | 23. _____ Music |

▷ Use the graph to answer.

| 24. What hobby was named most? _____ | 25. What hobby was named least? _____ |
| 26. How many more students named sports than video games?

 ☐ ___ more students | 27. How many more students named television than music?

 ☐ ___ more students |

▶Add. pages 24–29

1.   5
  + 3
	2. 9
	  + 6
		3. 37
		  + 12
			4. 76
			  + 16

5.   37
  + 26
	6. 578
	  + 164
		7. 366
		  + 249
			8. 4,525
			  + 734

▶Subtract. pages 30–35

9.   18
  – 9
	10. 15
	  – 8
		11. 36
		  – 21
			12. 74
			  – 46

13.   91
  – 74
	14. 482
	  – 191
		15. 577
		  – 368
			16. 1,425
			  – 642

▶Write each time two ways. pages 36–37

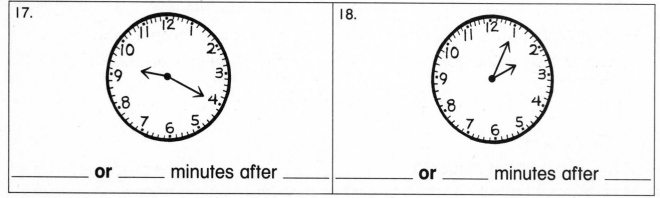

17. _____ **or** _____ minutes after _____

18. _____ **or** _____ minutes after _____

149

▶Use each table to make a graph.
pages 38–39

19. This table shows what
time of day the library helpers
in Read City like to work.

Favorite Work Times	
Morning	8
Afternoon	4
After School	6
Evening	2

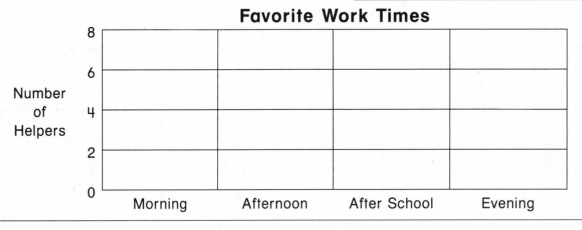

Favorite Work Times

20. Ms. Green made this table
to show what times of day
people use the library.

Times People Use the Library	
Morning	20
Afternoon	30
After School	40
Evening	10

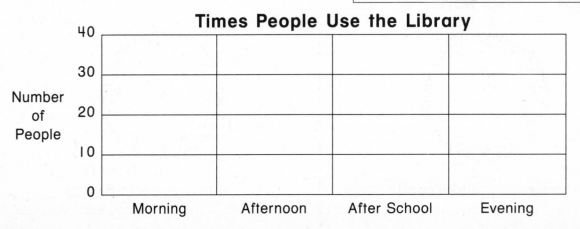

Times People Use the Library

Extra Practice

▷ Multiply.

pages 46–49			
1. $\begin{array}{r} 9 \\ \times\,0 \\ \hline \end{array}$	2. $\begin{array}{r} 8 \\ \times\,3 \\ \hline \end{array}$	3. $\begin{array}{r} 2 \\ \times\,1 \\ \hline \end{array}$	4. $\begin{array}{r} 7 \\ \times\,4 \\ \hline \end{array}$

pages 50–51			
5. $\begin{array}{r} 9 \\ \times\,5 \\ \hline \end{array}$	6. $\begin{array}{r} 3 \\ \times\,6 \\ \hline \end{array}$	7. $\begin{array}{r} 6 \\ \times\,5 \\ \hline \end{array}$	8. $\begin{array}{r} 8 \\ \times\,6 \\ \hline \end{array}$

pages 52–57			
9. $\begin{array}{r} 2 \\ \times\,7 \\ \hline \end{array}$	10. $\begin{array}{r} 8 \\ \times\,8 \\ \hline \end{array}$	11. $\begin{array}{r} 4 \\ \times\,7 \\ \hline \end{array}$	12. $\begin{array}{r} 9 \\ \times\,7 \\ \hline \end{array}$
13. $\begin{array}{r} 5 \\ \times\,7 \\ \hline \end{array}$	14. $\begin{array}{r} 4 \\ \times\,8 \\ \hline \end{array}$	15. $\begin{array}{r} 7 \\ \times\,8 \\ \hline \end{array}$	16. $\begin{array}{r} 8 \\ \times\,9 \\ \hline \end{array}$

▷ Write each time two ways. pages 58–59

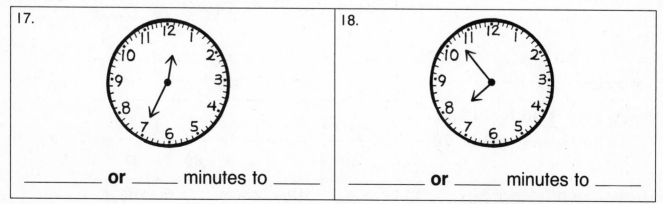

17. _____ **or** _____ minutes to _____

18. _____ **or** _____ minutes to _____

Round to the nearest ten.
pages 60–61

19. It took 43 days for a seed to become a flower.
    Is that nearer to 40 or 50?

    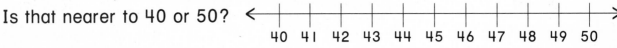

    It is nearer to _____.

20. Gail planted 37 rose bushes.
    Is that nearer to 30 or 40?

    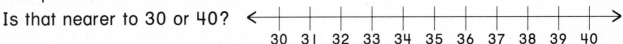

    It is nearer to _____.

21. Carl used 69 buckets of water to water the plants.
    Is that nearer to 60 or 70?

    It is nearer to _____.

22. Steve planted 14 different types of vegetables.
    Is it nearer to 10 or 20?

    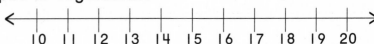

    It is nearer to _____.

23. A hose is 85 feet long.
    Is it nearer to 80 or 90?

    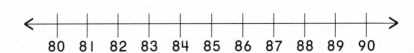

    It is nearer to _____.

▷Multiply.

pages 76–79			
1. 60 × 4	2. 300 × 3	3. 13 × 3	4. 11 × 8
pages 80–83 5. 17 × 5	6. 36 × 2	7. 24 × 7	8. 73 × 5
pages 84–85 9. 243 × 3	10. 176 × 2	11. 315 × 3	12. 181 × 2
pages 86–87 13. 427 × 6	14. 135 × 8	15. 519 × 3	16. 711 × 7

▷Ring A.M. or P.M.   pages 88–89

17. John cleans his room at 2:30.   A.M.   P.M.

18. Ruth eats breakfast at 6:45.   A.M.   P.M.

19. Frank watches an afternoon program at 3:45.   A.M.   P.M.

20. The sun rises.   A.M.   P.M.

Extra Practice

▷Round to the nearest ten.
Estimate to solve.
pages 90–91

---

21. The school play had 3 acts.
Each act was 24 minutes long.
About how many minutes long
was the play?

$$
\begin{array}{r}
24 \\
\times\ 3 \\
\hline
\end{array}
\longrightarrow
\begin{array}{r}
\boxed{} \\
\times\ 3 \\
\hline
\end{array}
$$

about $\boxed{}$ minutes

22. There were 36 rows of seats
in the lunchroom. Each row
had 9 seats. About how many
seats in all were there?

$$
\begin{array}{r}
36 \\
\times\ 9 \\
\hline
\end{array}
\longrightarrow
\begin{array}{r}
\boxed{} \\
\times\ 9 \\
\hline
\end{array}
$$

about $\boxed{}$ seats

---

23. The set crew made a fake brick
wall. It had 5 rows of bricks with
34 bricks in each row. About
how many bricks were used?

$$
\begin{array}{r}
34 \\
\times\ 5 \\
\hline
\end{array}
\longrightarrow
\begin{array}{r}
\boxed{} \\
\times\ 5 \\
\hline
\end{array}
$$

about $\boxed{}$ bricks

24. There were 261 students in
the school. Each student got
3 tickets. About how many
tickets in all were there?

$$
\begin{array}{r}
261 \\
\times\ 3 \\
\hline
\end{array}
\longrightarrow
\begin{array}{r}
\boxed{} \\
\times\ 3 \\
\hline
\end{array}
$$

about $\boxed{}$ tickets

---

25. Mr. Hall bought trim for
6 costumes. Each costume had
18 yards of trim. About how
many yards did Mr. Hall Buy?

$$
\begin{array}{r}
18 \\
\times\ 6 \\
\hline
\end{array}
\longrightarrow
\begin{array}{r}
\boxed{} \\
\times\ 6 \\
\hline
\end{array}
$$

about $\boxed{}$ yards

26. There were 23 students. Each
student made 2 dozen cookies
to sell at the play. How many
dozens of cookies in all did
they make?

$$
\begin{array}{r}
23 \\
\times\ 2 \\
\hline
\end{array}
\longrightarrow
\begin{array}{r}
\boxed{} \\
\times\ 2 \\
\hline
\end{array}
$$

about $\boxed{}$ dozen

154

Extra Practice

▷Divide.

pages 98–101			
1. $6\overline{)24}$	2. $4\overline{)20}$	3. $3\overline{)12}$	4. $5\overline{)15}$
pages 102–103			
5. $7\overline{)28}$	6. $7\overline{)35}$	7. $7\overline{)56}$	8. $7\overline{)49}$
pages 104–105			
9. $8\overline{)16}$	10. $8\overline{)48}$	11. $8\overline{)56}$	12. $8\overline{)64}$
pages 106–109			
13. $9\overline{)9}$	14. $9\overline{)36}$	15. $9\overline{)54}$	16. $9\overline{)72}$

▷What time will it be? pages 110–111

17. 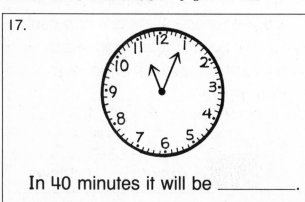 In 40 minutes it will be _____.	18. 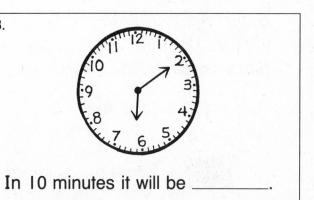 In 10 minutes it will be _____.

▷Ring the correct problem.
pages 112–113

---

19. Terese stacked cans of soup at a store. She made 6 rows with 18 cans in each row. How many cans of soup in all were there?

$$\begin{array}{r} 18 \\ \times\ 6 \\ \hline 108 \end{array} \text{ cans}$$

$$6\overline{)18} \quad \overset{3}{} \text{ cans}$$

---

20. Carol had 35 plants. She put them in rows with 7 plants in each row. How many rows of plants did Carol have?

$$\begin{array}{r} 35 \\ \times\ 7 \\ \hline 245 \end{array} \text{ rows}$$

$$7\overline{)35} \quad \overset{5}{} \text{ rows}$$

---

21. Ichiro had 21 homework problems. He had 3 nights to finish his homework. How many problems should Ichiro solve each night?

$$\begin{array}{r} 21 \\ \times\ 3 \\ \hline 63 \end{array} \text{ problems}$$

$$3\overline{)21} \quad \overset{7}{} \text{ problems}$$

---

22. The school cooks baked 6 pans of bars. Each pan made 42 bars. How many bars in all did they bake?

$$\begin{array}{r} 42 \\ \times\ 6 \\ \hline 252 \end{array} \text{ bars}$$

$$6\overline{)42} \quad \overset{7}{} \text{ bars}$$

---

23. Tara walks 3 miles every day. How many miles does Tara walk in 30 days?

$$\begin{array}{r} 30 \\ \times\ 3 \\ \hline 90 \end{array} \text{ miles}$$

$$3\overline{)30} \quad \overset{10}{} \text{ miles}$$

▷ Divide.

pages 120–123			
1. $5\overline{)31}$	2. $4\overline{)33}$	3. $4\overline{)40}$	4. $8\overline{)800}$
pages 124–127			
5. $2\overline{)48}$	6. $3\overline{)39}$	7. $2\overline{)25}$	8. $3\overline{)67}$
pages 128–131			
9. $3\overline{)44}$	10. $4\overline{)71}$	11. $6\overline{)314}$	12. $5\overline{)418}$

▷ Write the answer. pages 132–133

13. It takes 30 minutes to get to Susan's aunt's house.
Susan and her family leave at 4:10 P.M.
What time will they get to Susan's aunt's house?

They will get there at _____ P.M.

Start Time

▷Ring the correct problem.
pages 134–135

---

14. A plane has 150 seats.
There are 6 seats in a row.
How many rows of seats
does the plane have?

$$\begin{array}{r} 150 \\ \times\ 6 \\ \hline 900 \end{array} \text{ rows}$$

$$6\overline{)150} \quad 25 \text{ rows}$$

---

15. The restaurant had 132 tables and
3 waiters. Each waiter served
the same number of tables. How
many tables did each waiter serve?

$$\begin{array}{r} 132 \\ \times\ 3 \\ \hline 396 \end{array} \text{ tables}$$

$$3\overline{)132} \quad 44 \text{ tables}$$

---

16. There are 240 rooms at Sleep Inn
Hotel. Each room has 2 beds. How
many beds in all are there?

$$\begin{array}{r} 240 \\ \times\ 2 \\ \hline 480 \end{array} \text{ beds}$$

$$2\overline{)240} \quad 120 \text{ beds}$$

---

17. There are 240 rooms on 6 floors
at Sleep Inn Hotel. How many
rooms are there on each floor?

$$\begin{array}{r} 240 \\ \times\ 6 \\ \hline 1{,}440 \end{array} \text{ rooms}$$

$$6\overline{)240} \quad 40 \text{ rooms}$$

---

18. A farmer has planted 175 rows of
corn with 5 corn plants in each
row. How many plants
does the farmer have?

$$\begin{array}{r} 175 \\ \times\ 5 \\ \hline 875 \end{array} \text{ plants}$$

$$5\overline{)175} \quad 35 \text{ plants}$$
